CW01620105

NEWTON PAGE

NEWTON PAGE

CHARLES DICKENS

THE MISER BOOKS

Merryweather's Lives and Anecdotes of Misers

NEWTON PAGE

NEWTON PAGE

Published by Newton Page

Charles Dickens: The Miser Books

Merryweather's Lives and Anecdotes of Misers

www.newtonpage.com

Published by Newton Page 2015

1 3 5 7 9 10 8 6 4 2

ISBN 978-1-934619-13-1

Printed in the United States of America
Set in Adobe Garamond Pro

CONTENTS

DEDICATION

This book is dedicated to the memory of the 'miser' and founder of Guy's Hospital in London:

Thomas Guy
(1644-1724)

In life, he was mercelessly ridiculed by the public for his self-denial, economy and selflessness. But in death, his legacy has ceaselessly continued to support the wellbeing of the poor and sick descendants of the very people who ridiculed him.

NOTE ON THE TEXT

Since Merryweather's *Lives and Anecdotes of Misers* was first published over one hundred and sixty years ago, conventions of spelling, grammar, punctuation, expression, vocabulary and general notation have each undergone considerable modernization. In addition, the relatively crude practices of mid nineteenth-century book production have been gradually replaced by the radically more exacting standards of modern publishing, which demand both uniformity of typesetting and editorial consistency. As a consequence of those changes, the modern reader is used to a more polished product than those available in the 1850s.

However, notwithstanding the usual expectations of the modern reader, and in full appreciation that the original texts are not as easy on the modern eye as they would have been on the mid nineteenth-century equivalent, the temptation to edit them to conform with modern writing and publishing conventions has been resisted. That approach has been taken because to do anything other than retain the original form of the book would be to detract from its colorful character.

F. Somner Merryweather originally wrote *Lives and Anecdotes of Misers* for the consideration of the inhabitants of Great Britain. As such, it is tailored to conform with the conventional nineteenth-century stylistic expectations of a British readership.

American readers will notice that in maintaining the integrity of the original publication, the original historic British forms of spelling have been retained. More generally, readers will notice both inconsistent and imaginative forms of spelling throughout.

This book has been based on the earliest available edition of: *Lives and Anecdotes of Misers; Or the Passion of Avarice Displayed: in the Parsimonious Habits, Unaccountable Lives and Remarkable Deaths of the Most Notorious Misers of All Ages, With a Few Words on Frugality and Saving.* London: Simpkin, Marshall, and Co., Stationers' Court, Paternoster Row (1850).

PREFACE

PREFACE

If the poet said true, when he wrote that the proper study of mankind is man, the subject of this little volume will serve some better object than mere curiosity. It has been my aim throughout its compilation, to render it a volume of instruction as well as of amusement. I think it a pleasant way to instil a moral by exciting curiosity, and have endeavoured, in gathering together examples of avarice, to show the evils of that passion—to show how, before its influence, vanish the better spirits of the heart, and how impossible it is, that within the avaricious soul, virtue or charity can find a profitable habitation.

In presenting this volume to the public, I deem it but justice to myself, and candour to my readers, to intimate that I do not profess to fill the book with novel and unheard-of instances of avarice. I have not sought, like a diligent antiquary, into the biographical minutiae of misers. I have not met with any old manuscript lives; I have discovered in public libraries no curious diary of a miser's schemes, or of a miser's gains. Some of these materials have been in print before, and have doubtless long ago, amused many of my readers; but a great proportion have been extracted from books but little known—from forgotten pamphlets, and from newspapers long out of date. Some have been gathered from old country gossips, and some have been gleaned from ephemeral sources, to which I cannot even myself distinctly refer. I have thought it fit to declare thus much, lest, in introducing some anecdote which my readers may have heard of before, they should accuse me of plagiarism. I would have it remembered too, that old illustrations maybe so re-applied, as that the life of a Daniel Dancer, or of a John Elwes, may still carry a warning, of how sinful is avarice, or of how fruitless is an eternal parsimony; although they may have been related in other books.

My instances are veritable ones, and most of them I believe to be illustrations of real life unexaggerated by fiction. Whilst I have an object in the compilation—whilst I aim, to point now and then a moral, and to exemplify sometimes one of the propensities of the human mind, I have not forgotten that many will read the book to drive away ennui; and that youthful readers in winter evenings may expect some amusement from my pages. As I earnestly wish that such may be the case, I have endeavoured, in choosing my illustrations and anecdotes, to select those which appeared the most amusing from their eccentricity, or the most instructive by the warning they convey. I have winnowed my multitudinous materials from all those anecdotes and reminiscences, which from the coarseness of their allusions, or the indelicacy of their nature, might seem offensive to virtue, or likely to prove dangerous to innocence.

I hope then, the book may not be without its use, and am inclined to say, as Southey said on one occasion,

Be it with thee according to thy worth;
Go, little book! in faith I send thee forth.

or in the quaint words of a very old author, whose book I happened just now to take down from my shelf, would say—

Go thou little book, with due reverence
And with an humble heart; recommend me
To all those, who of their benevolence

This little Treatise doth read, hear, or see,
Wherewith I pray them contented to be,
And to amend it, in places behovable,
Wherein I have faulted, or be culpable.
For hard it is, a man to attain
To make a thing perfect, at the first sight;
But when it is read, and well over seen
Faults may be found, that never came to light,
Though the maker do his diligence and might.
Praying them to take it, as I have intended,
And to forgive one, if I have offended.

F. S. M.

Gloucester Place.

Kentish Town.

CHAPTER I

AVARICE DESCRIBED AND EXEMPLIFIED.

Description of this Passion by Ancient Writers—Dion the Philosopher—Euripides—Aristotle—Plato—Anecdote of Alcibiades—Boethius—Sir George Mackenzie on this Passion—Anecdote from Horace—Avarice in a Cardinal and in a Pope—The Miser described by Old Burton; by Dryden; by Goldsmith; by Robert Pollok—Avarice in History—Analogy between Avarice and Prodigality—A Curious Anecdote—Avarice in the Great and "Noble"—The Great Duke of Marlborough—Another Ducal Miser of a more Modern Day—A Little Rustic and a Great Duke—The Insatiableness of Acquisitiveness—Jemmy Wood of Gloucester—Osterval and Danden both starved to Death—Strength and Durability of the Passion of Avarice—Virtue not quite Extinct—Benevolence and Parsimony often displayed by the same Individual—Guyot, a reputed Miser of Marseilles; his singular Will—An unexpected Contribution to a good Work, &c. &c.

AVARICE DESCRIBED AND EXEMPLIFIED.

Although a passion so common to mankind, there is none that has received such scorn and contempt, as that of avarice. Philosophers and poets of all ages, and of every nation, have exerted their wit and satire, to denounce, and expose, the evils of this ungodly lust. Moralists have declared this passion for gold and silver the most unpardonable, because the most detestable, of all passions. "There are men," exclaims an ancient satirist, "who do not profit to live, but who seem to live, for no other purpose than to gain." The denunciations of classic eloquence have been hurled against it. Heathens regarded it as a sin, the possession of which would exclude them from the favor of the gods. "Avarice," says Dion, the philosopher, "is the source of all wickedness." It was the opinion of the high-minded Euripides that an avaricious man could neither think nor desire, any good thing; and Lucilius, the friend of Scipio Africanus, does not forget to employ the pen of satire against this base and grovelling passion. "A miser," he writes, "is good to nobody, because he is wicked to himself." Plautus, in his character of Euclio, has graphically pourtrayed the meanness of avarice; nor can we even say that he exaggerates when he makes his miser repine, that he cannot save the smoke from his own miserable fire. "The lust of riches," says Aristotle, "is without end. Riches make a covetous man poor; for his avarice will not allow him to employ, for fear of losing them." Plato, the philosopher, once advised a miser, that if he was desirous of becoming truly rich, not to strive to increase his wealth, but to decrease his avarice—advice worthy of that great man. Valerius speaks of a miser who, in a famine, sold a mouse for two hundred pence, and died of starvation.[1] It was a keen rebuke with which Socrates humbled the pride of avarice in a wealthy ancient. Alcibiades, the great Athenian general, was boasting to the philosopher of the extent of his land, and the immensity of his riches. The stoic laid before the proud man a map of the world. "Pray," said he, "show me where your land lyeth here?" The point of a pin would have covered all! "Though the rich miser," says Boethius, "should be in a flowing whirlpool of gold, he could not satisfy his appetite for wealth; let him adorn his neck with the berries of the Red Sea, and cleave his rich soils with a hundred oxen!" We might extract some curious anecdotes of misers from the lore of classic ages. Horace speaks of a man named Ovid, who was so abundantly rich that he could measure his gold and silver by bushels, and yet was so penurious that he would go almost naked about the streets, never eating enough to satisfy the demands of hunger. Fearing lest he should fall into poverty, he lived most wretchedly all his life.

Our old English writers have not been less severe in delineating the evils of avarice. "It is," says Brown in his Religio Medici, "not so much a vice as a species of madness." "I must beg rich and avaricious men's leave," says Sir George Mackenzie, "to laugh as much at their folly, as I should do at a shepherd who would weep and grieve, because his master would give him no more beasts to herd; or at a steward because his lord gave him no more servants to feed. Nor can I think a man who, having gained a great estate, is afraid to live comfortably upon it, less ridiculous, than I would do him, who having built a convenient,

1. Lib. 7. cap. Vi

or it may be a stately house, should choose to walk in the rain, or expose himself to storms, lest he should defile or profane the floor of his almost idolized rooms." Pontanus speaks of a cardinal who was so extraordinarily avaricious, that he would often disguise himself as a poor slave, or groom, and steal away the corn from his own horses. Many of the vices of the popes—and history tells us they were not a few—sprang from their lust for gold. The sins of Boniface the Eighth, of whom it was said that "he crept into the popedom like a fox, ruled like a lion, and died like a dog," were principally the sins of avarice. We may illustrate his craft and avarice by an anecdote. In the year 1297 the Franciscans were anxious to obtain from this pope a bull of privileges, for which they offered him forty thousand ducats. The pope inquired if they had the money ready; they answered that they had, and that it was then at Rome in the hands of a certain banker, whom they named. He desired three days to consider the matter, at the end of which time they were requested to return. In the interval, the pope sent to the banker, and demanded the money which the holy friars had lodged in his hands; and in order to quiet the conscience of the Italian money changer, he accompanied this demand with an absolution for his breach of trust. When the three days were expired, the Franciscans waited upon his "holiness," fully anticipating success. The successor of Saint Peter received them graciously, but told them that on due consideration he could not grant their request, as it was opposed to the rule of Saint Francis; but, as to the money—why, it must remain for the use of the holy see!

Old Burton, with his usual learning, describes the characteristics of the miser. "He is commonly sad," says he, "as Ahab's spirit was, because he could not get Naboth's vineyard; and if he lay out his money at any time, though it be to necessary uses, to his own children's good, he brawls and scolds, his heart is heavy, much disquieted he is, and loth to part from it. He is of a wearish, dry, pale constitution, and cannot sleep for cares, and worldly business; 'his riches,' saith Solomon, 'will not let him sleep;' or if he do sleep, it is of a very unquiet, interrupt, unpleasing sleep, with his bags in his arms; and though he be at a banquet, or some merry feast, he sighs for grief of heart; his wearish body takes no rest; he is troubled in his abundance, and sorrowful in plenty; unhappy in the present, and more unhappy in the life to come. He is a perpetual drudge; restless in his thoughts, and never satisfied; a slave—a wretch—a dust worm, still seeking what sacrifice he may offer to his golden god!" Dryden sums up the misery of avarice in a few lines; he says,

Content is wealth, the riches of the mind,
And happy he who can that treasure find;
But the base miser starves amidst his store,
Broods on his gold; and griping still for more,
Sits sadly pining, and believes he's poor!

And Goldsmith, in his graphic and charming way, thus refers to the insatiable nature of this unholy passion:

As some lone miser visiting his store,
Bends at his treasure, counts, recounts it o'er;
Hoards after hoards, his rising raptures fill,
Yet still he sighs, for hoards are wanting still.

Molière in his "L'Avare," and Shadwell in his "Miser," have both attempted to display the workings of avarice by dramatic representation. Far from exaggerating, their characters fall short of the reality, and have all been surpassed by the examples of niggardly saving, and penury, given to us in the lives of Daniel Dancer, John Elwes, Jemmy Taylor, and their eccentric clan. Robert Pollok, the author of "The Course of Time," thus paints in words the miser at his store:

But there was one in folly further gone;
With eye awry, incurable, and wild,
The laughing stock of devils and of men,
And by his guardian angel quite given up—
The miser, who with dust inanimate
Held wedded intercourse. Ill guided wretch!
Thou might'st have seen him at the midnight hour,
When good men slept, and in light winged dreams
Ascended up to God—in wasteful hall,
With vigilance and fasting worn to skin
And bone, and wrapped in most debasing rags:
Thou might'st have seen him bending o'er his heaps,
And holding strange communion with his gold;
And as his thievish fancy seemed to hear
The nightman's foot approach, starting alarmed;
And in his old, decrepit, withered hand,
That palsy shook, grasping the yellow earth
To make it sure. Of all God made upright,
And in their nostrils breathed a living soul,
Most fallen, most prone, most earthy, most debased.
Of all that sold Eternity for Time,
None bargained on so easy terms for death.
Illustrious fool! nay, most inhuman wretch!
He sat among his bags, and, with a look
Which hell might be made ashamed of, drove the poor
Away unalmsed; and 'midst abundance died—

Sorest of evils—died of utter want!

If we were disposed to do so, it would be no difficult task to show the powerful influence of avarice upon the rise and progress of nations, and it would be instructive to comment, with the annals of our country before us, upon the working of this passion, in the history of the English people. We should observe, in the origin of those wars and tumults, which incessantly employed the arms, and fed the turbulent passions of our early kings, the grim features of avarice. We should behold in the tyranny and oppression of monarchs over their people, the power of the same greedy and selfish lust, and we should find the corruptions, and abominations, of the old popish church, to have sprang from the love of gold. The most glaring evils of society, and the grossest corruptions of religion, were instigated and supported by the promptings of avarice. Monarchs, ravenous to acquire, looked enviously at rival kingdoms; the more they obtained, the more did they demand. The miseries of war, the slaughter of legions of their subjects were as nothing, when opposed to their schemes of avarice and ambition. It was the treasures which the parsimony of the Jews accumulated that excited in old England the cupidity of Norman power. Christian kings and Israelitish money-lenders were alike greedy after wealth; and we all know what massacres and plundering arose from this love of gold. It was the avarice of monks and popish priests that excited the envy of Henry Tudor. In their case the love of gold was the root of all evil, as regarded their own interests at least; for had the monks adhered to their ancient rules of poverty, and prayer; their monasteries would not have been so zealously suppressed.

The passion of avarice has various manifestations; one craves for money but to hoard it in his chests, others crave for money to spend it in their selfish pleasures. Thus it is that avarice is sometimes found in the spendthrift, and thus it is that spendthrifts so often become inveterate misers. Perhaps the best illustration of this feeling is in the parsimony and extravagance which we sometimes observe combined in gamesters. Did we want a fearful lesson, we would go to the gaming table to behold the demon of avarice in his triumph—the haggard face—the feverish brow—the eager anxious eye—the nervous twitches of the mouth, and the clenching of the hands, are the outward signs of the fierce and deadly struggle within. The transition, indeed, from prodigality to avarice is so easy, that one would almost feel inclined to regard the spendthrift, greedy for sensual enjoyment and riotous pleasure, as only exhibiting another manifestation of avarice; it is a species of that same covetous feeling, longing to enjoy a greater portion of pleasure than usually falls to the lot of man: it is selfishness; and selfishness is next akin to avarice. A young man of vicious principles squandered in a few years a sumptuous fortune. His houses and his lands had one by one, and piece by piece, been forfeited to gamblers, or sold to gratify his profligacy. His fortune gone, and no longer possessing the means of dissipation, he found his companions desert him; he had treated them liberally during his mad career; they had feasted at his table, and drunk plenteously of his wine; but companions in sensual joys are seldom grateful or sincere in their friendship. Forsaken and alone, he began to despair, and formed a resolution, which when formed few, in the adversity of fortune, have the courage to resist—he resolved to terminate with his own hand, a life which he deemed no longer desirable, and in which he could see no further source of happiness. He left his home in this suicidal mind, and wandering about, he came almost unconsciously to the brow of an eminence, which looked down upon what were lately his estates. He threw himself upon the ground, and for the first time for many years began to meditate. It was a good spirit that was now struggling in the future miser, before which the demon of suicide fled.

He sat for hours in that brown study, and he arose an altered and determined man. He had formed a resolution that all those fair lands should be his again. He walked hastily forward, determined to avail himself of the first opportunity of earning money that presented itself; and when he had obtained it, he resolved to use it with rigid parsimony. He had conquered during those few hours of reflection every feeling of pride, and his first attempt to earn money was a sufficient test of the sincerity of this triumph. He saw a heap of coals shot out of a cart, on the pavement before a house; he offered to shovel them into the cellar; his services were accepted, and remunerated with a trifling sum; yet trifling as it was, he resolved to save the greatest portion. He embraced every means of obtaining money, and did not allow himself to consider the meanness or servility of the occupation. Everything that could be applied to a use he hoarded up, and when accumulated sold. By these means, step by step, and little by little, after years of patient labour, he saved enough to purchase a few cattle; these he improved, and after awhile sold at a profit. During all this time he practiced the strictest parsimony, and he was ultimately enabled, by his accumulations, to recover his lost estates. Parsimony such as this we should feel disposed to excuse, but the result in his case, it is said, was disastrous, for parsimony became, by long habit, confirmed into avarice, and the man died a scraping, grasping miser, with sixty thousand pounds in his money chests.

It is not always that avarice assumes the garb of wretchedness; it is not always that the miser appears to the public eye, a lank and half starved wretch, with loathsome rags upon his shoulders. The passion is sometimes associated with men, whose names have been renowned for great actions, and for vast achievements in the world. That great warrior, the Duke of Marlborough, allowed the promptings of avarice to tarnish a flame designed to live for centuries. Many and disreputable are the charges of peculation which have been advanced against him, and numerous are the anecdotes remembered by tradition, or recorded in books, of his pinching parsimony. When the clouds were gathering in the heavens, and infirmity had warned him of coming dissolution, he would walk from the public room in Bath to his lodgings, in a cold dark night, through wind and rain, to save sixpence for coach hire. Yet that great general left at his death a fortune of more than a million and a half of money, which, as if to show to others the folly of such meanless parsimony, was inherited by a grandson of Lord Trevors, who had been one of his bitterest enemies. But we need not go back so far to find noble misers; some of the members of our proud nobility of to day, afford striking examples of parsimony and avarice in the great. We have known some whose riches are so great, that they may be compared with the riches of Croesus; grumble over their tradesmen's bills, and haggle for an hour to obtain the reduction of a shilling, did not interest prompt the tradesman sooner to submit, in hopes of future "patronage," from such distinguished and noble personages. If the reader will take the trouble to enquire, he may glean some curious anecdotes of a "noble" miser, of the present day, whose parsimony is so great, that he deprives his domestics of their perquisites, and has been known to have sold the refuse fat from his own kitchen for the trifle which it produced. This descendant of a valiant race may be seen, in the locality of his own mansion, with a huge basket on his arm, wandering from shop to shop, and from stall to stall, to pick up bargains or thrifty provender for his household. He not only attends to the economy of his kitchen, but even to the most minute affairs of his farm; his dairy receives no small share of his attention, and he will sometimes condescend to measure out, and sell his milk in retail, to the neighbouring villagers. One morning, it is related, a little girl presented herself at the castle, and giving in her jug and penny, was served by his grace, who, pleased with her appearance, gave the little damsel a kiss, telling her at the same time that she would always now be able to say, that she had been kissed by a duke. "Yes," replied the little rustic, "but you took the penny, though!" "We could point to many such instances of aristocratic penury, but we do not wish to draw our illustrations from contemporary characters.

The total absence of all ulterior motive in the parsimony of the miser is a convincing proof of how powerful are the cravings of acquisitiveness, when unduly excited. "If a miser be the owner of fifty acres," said Dr. Combe, "it will give him delight to acquire fifty more; if of one thousand, or one hundred thousand, he will still be gratified in adding to this number. His understanding may be convinced that he already possesses ample store for any enjoyment, and abundant to provide against every want; yet if this faculty be active, he will feel his joys impaired if he cease to amass." The ever famous Jemmy Wood, of Gloucester, who died worth nearly two millions of money, did not cease to go on accumulating wealth after he had obtained more than he or his family could spend in their lifetime, if they spent with common prudence. But the propensity to acquire, when unduly active, absorbs all other powers and motives of the human mind. The love of accumulating gold is so intense that it defies all fear of death, and the being whose will is submissive to its dictates, would calmly look starvation in the face; and rather than invade his hoards to purchase a few extra comforts for the body, expire by lingering and slow degrees. Ostervald, the miser, died, because he would not spend a few shillings in the purchase of a little soup; and Danden, the miser, of Berlin, positively died of starvation, whilst he had secreted under his floor twenty thousand crowns in specie. He had no heir but a brother, with whom he had been at enmity for seven and thirty years, because he had once sent him a letter without paying the postage. Yet this sordid wretch was a man of intellectual talent, and a master of languages. "True it is," as Dr. Combe asserts, "that when the pursuit of wealth becomes the chief business of life, acquisitiveness engrosses the intellect, deadens the moral sentiments and debases the whole faculties of the mind."[2]

Other passions diminish in their strength, as age approaches. The sensual passions become palled by gratification. The sins of youth are forgotten, as the hair grows grey, and the eyes become dimmed with the film of age; but the passion of avarice, unlike other passions of the human mind, knows no satiety; it becomes strengthened by its gratification; it derives nourishment from its very excesses, and, like the sturdy oak, becomes stronger as its age increases. It is difficult to discover the motives of hoary avarice—with limbs bending beneath the weight of years—with hair blanched by the snows of many winters—sans sight—sans teeth—sans everything—yet gloating over gold which he can never live to want, and greedy for acquisitions which can procure no happiness. We can only imagine that the mind, so absorbed by avarice, is rendered imbecile to all other feelings; or that the thoughts become so engrossed in their mammon worship, as to forget the flight of years, and the phantom of the tomb! And yet, perhaps, even the worst passions of the human mind are incapable of extinguishing all semblance of a better nature. Some slight trace of virtue— some lingering remains of charity—some indications of benevolence, will lie slumbering in the heart, although the calculations of avarice, and the audacity of crime, may have buried those feelings, and incased them as in the grave. The heart of the miser—of the robber—of even the murderer; if studied with intense scrutiny—if probed with skill, will not be found totally impregnable. Vice may have contaminated the stream of thought, and guarded the heart with the watchfulness of a fiend; but there is no breast

2. System of Phrenology, vol. i. p.318.

so besieged, that the angel of goodness may not redeem;—no heart, some avenue of which may not be surprised—no nature so obdurate, to which some good feeling or sentiment of love, may not appeal. Even where sin has most contaminated the heart, and excited the evil passions of the human mind, there is some trait of humanity still left to emulate the philanthropist to exertion, and to inspire the blackest sinner with the sunshine of hope.

What is more anomalous in nature than the mind of man? Sometimes passions and sentiments, diametrically opposite in their nature, are found existing in the same individual. Ferocity and tenderness—revenge and love—parsimony and charity grow up, and are made manifest side by side. Nothing, perhaps, has won so much for the philosophy of Gall and Spurzheim as this singular fact, for nothing seems to demonstrate so clearly the innateness of our ideas and capacities. The education or peculiar mental training that would tend to develope a grasping pinching parsimony, certainly does not appear to us the kind of training to implant principles of benevolence, and charity; in the human heart. And yet, perhaps, in these very anomalies, if we closely examine, we shall find a spirit of harmony, one propensity will seem to prompt and call into activity another feeling; the virtue becomes the excuse for the vice, and the mind is lulled by the gratification of two of its most opposite, but most powerful propensities, till the bad man thinks his motives good, and looks with complacency upon his evil deeds. We have a curious anecdote of the combination of parsimony with charity, to illustrate our meaning, and to show how a sordid vice is made by some subservient to their schemes of benevolence and love. We willingly forget the vice, and call it self-denial, whilst dwelling upon the munificence of the virtue.

Some years ago, there lived in Marseilles an old man of the name of Guyot; he was known to every inhabitant, and every urchin in the streets could point him out as a niggard in his dealings, and a wretch of the utmost penury in his habits of life. From his boyhood, this old man had lived in the City of Marseilles, and, although the people treated him with scorn and disgust, nothing could induce him to leave it. When he walked the streets he was followed by a crowd of boys, who, hating him as a grasping miser, hooted him vociferously—insulted him with the coarsest epithets, and sometimes annoyed him by casting stones and filth at his person. There was no one to speak a kind word in his favour—no one to bestow an act of friendship, or a nod of recognition upon Guyot. He was regarded by all as an avaricious, griping old miser, whose whole life was devoted to the hoarding up of gold. At last this object of universal scorn died, and it was found that, by his parsimony, he had amassed an ample fortune. What was the surprise of his executors on opening his will, to find these remarkable words:—"Having observed, from my infancy, that the poor of Marseilles are ill supplied with water, which can only be procured at a great price, I have cheerfully laboured the whole of my life to procure for them this great blessing, and I direct that the whole of my property shall be expended in building an aqueduct for their use!"

When it was proposed to build Bethlehem Hospital, many benevolent individuals volunteered to solicit contributions by calling upon the inhabitants of London. Two of these gentlemen went to a small house in an impoverished neighbourhood; for the pence of the poor were solicited as well as the pounds of the rich. The door was open, and, as they drew nigh, they overheard an old man scolding his female servant for having thrown away a match, only one end of which had been used. Although so trivial a matter, the master appeared to be much enraged, and the collectors remained some- time outside the door, before the old man had finished his angry lecture. When the tones of his voice were somewhat subdued, they entered, and presenting themselves to this strict observer of frugality and saving, explained the object of their application; but they did not anticipate much success. The miser, however, for such he was reputed in the neighbourhood, no sooner understood their object, than he opened a closet, and bringing forth a well filled bag, counted therefrom four hundred guineas, which he presented to the astonished applicants. They expressed their surprise and thankfulness, and could not refrain from telling the old gentleman that they had overheard his quarrel with his domestic, and how little they expected, in consequence, to have met with such munificence from him. "Gentlemen," replied the old man, "your surprise is occasioned by my care of a thing, of such little consequence; but I keep my house, and save my money in my own way; my parsimony enables me to bestow more liberally in charity. With regard to benevolent donations, you may always expect most from prudent people who keep their own accounts, and who pay attention to trifles." When he had thus addressed them, he somewhat abruptly requested them to withdraw, and closed the door after them; thinking, perhaps, more of the match which his maid had so wantonly destroyed, than of the four hundred guineas which his benevolence had prompted him to bestow.

CHAPTER II

A FEW WORDS ON FRUGALITY AND SAVING.

Avarice the abuse of a feeling which God intended as a blessing—The virtue of Economy—Extravagance in literary Men—Parsimony versus Frugality—How to Save—The importance of little things—Jacob Clement the City Broker—Jacques Lafitte—The Dust Heap—Nothing useless—Marine Storekeepers—Mysterious Bone-pickers—Singular death of a Miser, &c., &c.

A FEW WORDS ON FRUGALITY AND SAVING.

Rather would we, that our pen fell powerless from our hand, than that we should inadvertently have said one word of discouragement to they who are striving, by cheerful and willing self-denial, to provide out of humble incomes a provision against the hour of misfortune. Because men will drink wine till they become no longer human—because men, in striving to degrade themselves to a level with beasts, forget all the responsibilities of their higher nature, and find delight in wallowing in oblivious drunkenness; we would not, on that account, refuse to partake with temperance of that which God has given us as a blessing. And because men forget their souls, and the nobler purposes of life, and in their eagerness and avarice for gold, root out all good and manly feeling, and coin, as it were, their very hearts into metal; we would not neglect, by prudent and honourable means, to acquire wealth. Whilst we abhore the abuse, and think it well to guard others by hideous examples of its folly and vice, we can appreciate and participate in its legitimate use. We look upon it as a solemn duty in men, whether regarded as citizens or as fathers of families, to practice a prudent economy; and the man who is frugal without being avaricious—who is parsimonious without being sordid—we regard as fulfilling one of his greatest, social duties. Joseph, be it remembered, was thought to display his sagacity when he advised Pharoah to lay up in the seven plenteous years, for the seven ensuing years of famine. "Where," said the king, "shall we find such an one as this? A man in whom is the spirit of God!" And St. Paul solemnly affirms that "he hath sunk even below infidelity, who is negligent to provide for those of his own house." If, therefore, economy is a virtue, wastefulness becomes a sin. And yet, how many weakly glory in being thought extravagant; ruined spendthrifts will boast of their meanless prodigality, and their wasteful dissipation, as if in their past liberal selfishness they could claim some forbearance for their present disrepute, or some compassion for the misfortunes into which their own heedlessness has thrown them. The learned, too, will disclaim all knowledge of the dull routine of economy, and proclaim their ignorance of the affairs of life, as if the confession endowed them with a virtue; but perfection is not the privilege of any order of men, and many who ought to have been the monitors of mankind, whose talents have made their names immortal, embittered their lives, and impaired the vigour of their intellects, by their thoughtless and wanton improvidence. The calamities of authors is a hackneyed theme. Savage, Steel, Sheridan, Gay, Logan, and Maginn, are not instances, as some have asserted, of literary misfortune and neglect, so much as examples of learned profligacy and imprudence. Most of them were at times affluent, and most of them had opportunities in the success and popularity of their writings, of providing means to ward off those calamities which darkened the annals of their literary history, and which made them so familiar with

"Want, the garret, and the jail."

We are too apt to overlook the difference which subsists between parsimony and avarice; the one, while it may be a virtue in some, is a sin in others; but avarice, in whomsoever it may appear, must always be regarded as a vice. Parsimony in the man who, having but a narrow income, is anxious to provide for his family, who is ambitious to ascend higher in the social scale; and who feels solicitous to save his progeny from some of those hard vicissitudes of poverty which his own experience has taught him to dread; parsimony in such an one becomes a virtue, worthy of our highest regard, and deserving our warmest approbation. It is kindled by the best feelings of nature, and the tenderest sympathies of the heart. It is a virtuous parsimony that seeks out of present affluence, to lay by something for a rainy day. It is an indication of a sinful avarice that would employ extortion, or use craft, and Israelitish cunning, to augment an already abundant store. It is a virtuous parsimony that would save a little to help an aged parent in the evening of life; to administer to the wants of the sick, or to provide the sad obsequies for poorer relatives. It is an indication of sinful avarice that would let the parent shiver over a fireless hearth, that would begrudge one atom of wealth to soothe the bed of sickness, or that would allow the charity of strangers to provide the last home for departed kindred. Avarice, indeed, is but a diseased action of a propensity, which, if properly used, is beneficial to our well being. The propensity to acquire is natural to the human mind, and when it is manifested by a prudent frugality, is one of the greatest moral blessings of life. Religion enjoins, and scripture warrants, the practice of economy, and

"Reason bids you for your own provide."—Pope.

The best and ablest writers of every age have proclaimed its benefits, and enforced it as a habit, which not only keeps poverty and want from humble homes, but inspires its observer with a feeling of manly independence and inward comfort, which greatly help to rob of their sting, the cares and vicissitudes of life. Whilst, therefore, in illustrating the passion of avarice, we have endeavoured to display by remarkable examples, the grovelling sordidness of that vice, we are anxious to distinguish between it, and its opposite virtue; as avarice is one of the most debasing propensities of the human mind, so is frugality one of its greatest virtues. Whilst one is the source of misery, wretchedness, and endless sin; the other is the promoter of domestic happiness, of homely comfort, and social joy.

Whilst, however, we applaud the economist, we detest the miser, and would willingly raise our voice, to aid the cry against the avaricious man; the cringing, grasping, selfish accumulator of gold, the cold, unfeeling, heartless money-lender. We would raise our voice against the greedy and the selfish, who would wrong the widow of her pittance, and who, whilst he possessed the means, would refuse to help the poor and indigent, with a fraction of his wealth. We would raise our voice, too, against that man, who, to increase his stores, would stoop to mean and grovelling acts, or sell his honour for a little gold. A heart so enshrined in mammon, is not worthy the society of upright men, and well deserves contempt. Reader! shun such when you meet with them; their very touch is contamination, and to seek their gold, is indeed to seek the wages of sin and death. It is hard that men will not always distinguish between wretches so worthless, and the honest, praiseworthy, frugal man. And yet, how often are the efforts of the latter discouraged by the unfeeling voice of the thoughtless prodigal, who laughs at his saving, and calls it parsimony; and at his frugality, and calls it avarice.

An ingenious writer compares a miser to a growing tree, which, whilst living and increasing, can be applied to no immediate use, but which at last, when cut down, supplies material for the most useful purposes; and a poet says, that

Riches, like insects, when conceal'd they lie,
Wait but for wings, and in their season fly.
Who sees pale Mammon pine amidst his store,
Sees but a backward steward of the poor;

This year a reservoir to keep and spare,
The next, a fountain, spouting through his heir.

Pope.

If this offers no palliation for the vice of avarice, it shows that the result of a miser's life, is at least, more profitable to mankind than that of the spendthrift. The miser treasures up his gold in his senseless fondness for the yellow metal: he cares not to put it out to interest or to invest it in commerce: he hoards it up, gloats over it in the day, and handles it in the dark at night. He sleeps with his bony fingers clenched about his bags, holding them tighter in his fitful dreams, lest the robbers, who are ever passing before him in his visions, should take his treasure from him. If the wind shakes his crazy habitation, the miser, with a sudden start, awakes:

"Along the silent room he stalks,
Looks back, and trembles as he walks.
Each lock, and every bolt, he tries,
In every creek and corner prys;
Then opes the chest, with treasure stor'd,
And stands in raptures o'er his hoard."

A being like this, who can help despising? But such an one bears no resemblance to the frugal man, whose object is merely to refrain from useless expenditure; and whilst participating with thankfulness in a few of the enjoyments, manifests no anxiety to revel in the superfluities of life till he has provided something to help him in adversity and decay.

With those who have no hereditary birthright before them—who have only their health and muscles for a fortune, and who, like the silkworm, must spin all their riches out of their own bosom—industry and frugality become, as we have said before, solemn duties, which they have no more right to neglect than they have to cast aside their implements of toil, and refuse to work for their daily bread: and yet how often do we see the artizan, with a numerous progeny, clustering around him, with a fond wife depending on his exertions, neglect, although he has ample opportunities, to lay by one penny to aid in the hour of sickness, or to help his family should death call him away. It is a bitter thought for a dying man, that they who crowd around his bed with anxious solicitude—they who for so many years he has loved and cherished—who have been a comfort to him in trouble, and a solace in the dark hour of adversity—that the dear being who has journied with him so cheerfully along the stony path of life, and who ever had a smile of hope for him, and a kind word to bless him when his soul was heavy—who always entered into his wishes, and sympathised with his emotions—whose warm and faithful heart, overflowing with a chaste and confiding love, was ever busy in scheming little plans to give him pleasure, and to anticipate his unuttered wishes: it is gall and bitterness to a dying man to think that this dear creature and his little ones should be left unprotected in the wide world alone—in the midst of unsympathising strangers, and the prospect of the workhouse as the only refuge from starvation. A bleak and torturing thought is that, to wring the expiring heart of a dyiag man! It is seldom, in- deed, that one who has passed his life so thoughtlessly, can enjoy that inward consolation, and that sustaining hope, which ought, at the moment of death, to fill the soul of a Christian: his anxious mind cannot untwine itself from its painful reveries, and he breathes his last without the peace of God that passeth all understanding.

We consider it, then, an imperative duty that all who have the power, should save—that they should husband up little by little an increasing store for their future wants. Some will say that, by doing this we are showing how little faith we have in Providence; but they that say so, speak unadvisedly, and might as well argue that, if we saw a child in the water, and could save it, we ought not to do so, but trust to Providence for its rescue. It is our duty to be provident, careful, and frugal: it is our duty, because the God of heaven bade us gather up the fragments that remain, and to allow nothing to be lost. We must not act, in this railway-stirring age, like the waggoner in the bog, but embrace the opportunities which God has given us, and use his gifts with prudence. Others will say, sufficient for the day is the evil thereof, and advise us to think less about what may happen to us by and bye; but they draw false reasoning from another holy passage, for if we become the humble instruments of our own preservation from pecuniary want, does that prove less our gratitude to Providence for having given us the means to do so? Yet this is a maxim, which, when indiscriminately applied, has sometimes wrought the ruin of many, both good and noble. James Ballantyne, the partner of Sir Walter Scott, on his death-bed, affirmed that many of those calamities which overtook them, and which involved the ruin of the great literary magician, was owing to the weakness of Scott in shrinking from the appearance of danger, and from his aptness to carry too far the maxim, that, "sufficient for the day is the evil thereof."

Many who have the wish to be frugal will scarcely know how to begin: they have lived so long the thoughtless spendthrift, that they cannot be thoughtful all at once. They will mention the trifling sum that forms their weekly earnings, and ask, how is it possible to reserve even a little, out of such a pittance? It is a cheerful proverb that tells us "Where there is a will there is a way;" and the homely truism is a suitable answer to all who ask, How can I save?

There are few working men who, if they have the desire to be economical, will not call to mind some useless luxury, in which they are in the habit of indulging, and from which they could easily refrain. Taste and caprice have invented an infinite variety of superficial wants, in these modem times, which are as unnecessary to our happiness, as some of them are injurious to our bodies. The morning glass, the evening pipe, or the Saturday's night revel, might be profitably dispensed with, both to the health and to the purse. The savings may not be great at first, but frugality will have gained the ascendancy; and it is astonishing how much prosperity will follow, and how many opportunities will offer, of adding to the little store, if prudence and industry are on the watch. Retrench, in every reasonable manner, your expences, and strictly adhere to the admirable axiom of the Roman poet—

"Infra Fortunam debet quisq; manere suam."—Ovid.

and recollect the words of Dr. Cotton, that

"Your portion is not large indeed,
But then, how little do you need,
For Nature's calls are few;
In this the Art of living lies,
To want no more than may suffice,
And make that little do."

There are few who have not, at one time or other, felt, how useful a few pounds would have proved, in advancing their future prospects; and who have not, at such times, looked back with regret to their past extravagance, and to their thoughtlessness, in spending stray sixpences. It is only when we count up such trivial sums, that we are convinced of their importance, or at all capable of judging how much we have lost by squandering them. The old tale of the poor drover, who gradually scraped enough together to purchase a calf, and, from that small beginning, went on until he became the possessor of many thousands a year, is an instance of frugality worth remembering; yet let it never be forgotten, that, "although the apprehensions of future wants may justify a cautious frugality, they can by no means excuse a sordid avarice." Bearing this in mind, the lives of misers, whilst they pourtray the evils of an inordinate passion to acquire, also illustrate a truism, well deserving the attention of all who are anxious to practice frugality without covetousness. The importance of little things, the value of trifles, and the power of the pence, is nowhere so strikingly exemplified, as in the habits of those eccentric characters, whose lives we have here presented to the reader. "Take care," said Lord Chesterfield, "of the pence, and the pounds will take care of themselves." The saying is worthy of remembrance; for small sums may, with some aptness, be compared to seconds of time, which generate years, centuries, and even eternity itself. Let not a regard for little things be thought a manifestation of avarice. Our Rothschilds, our Barings, and our Coutts', would never have amassed their almost fabulous fortunes, had they not constantly regarded little things, and looked well after the pence. Many of the most wealthy members of the Stock Exchange, who can now lend their thousands, and their tens of thousands, originally belonged to the most subordinate ranks of society. Jacob Clement, the city broker, who died a few years ago, leaving a fortune of three hundred thousand pounds, began life as a pot-boy at an inn, at Aylesbury. His first situation, in London, was as a waiter; but he had perseverance, practised frugality, and encouraged habits of saving; had he neglected such habits, he would probably have died a waiter. There is wisdom in that saying of the miser, who maintained, that "a farthing is the semina of wealth, the seed of a golden progeny;" and often has its truth been remembered, not only by misers, but by those whose virtues have only been equalled by their prosperity. Perhaps in no instance was this parsimonious care for trifles, so truly elevated into a virtue, as exemplified in the life of Jacques Laffitte. There appears something almost noble, in the pinching, screwing parsimony of that great banker. In an early month of the year 1778, with a tolerable education, and with many natural qualifications, for a financial life, Jacques Laffitte was seeking for a situation as a clerk. He had high hopes, and a light heart, for he brought with him a letter of introduction to M. Perregaux, the Swiss banker. But with all his sanguine anticipations, and golden day dreams, he was bashful, and retiring. It was with a trembling heart that the young provincial appeared before the Parisian man of bonds and gold; he managed to explain the purpose of his visit, and presented his letter of recommendation. The banker quietly read the note. "It is impossible," said he, as he laid it aside, "that I can find room for you at present; all my offices are full; should there be a vacancy at a future time, I will see what can be done; in the meantime, I advise yon to seek elsewhere, as it may be a considerable period before I shall be able to admit you." Away went sunshine, and prosperous visions! Disappointed and gloomy, poor Jacques left the presence of the polite banker. As he crossed, with downcast eyes, the courtyard of the noble mansion, he observed a pin lying on the ground; his habitual habits of frugality, amidst his disappointment, were still upon the watch; he picked up the pin, and carefully stuck it into the lapel of his coat. From that trivial action sprang his future greatness; that one single act of frugal care and regard for little things, opened the way to a stupendous fortune. From the window of his cabinet M. Perregaux had observed the action of the rejected clerk, and he wisely thought, that the man who would stoop to pick up a pin, under such circumstances, was endowed with the necessary qualities for a good economist; he read in that single act of parsimony, an indication of a great financial mind, and he deemed the acquisition of such an one as wealth itself.

Before the day had closed, Laffitte received a note from the banker. "A place," it said, "is made for you at my office, which you may take possession of to-morrow." The banker was not deceived in his estimate of the character of Laffitte, and the young clerk soon displayed a talent and aptness for his calling, that procured his advancement from the clerk to the cashier; from a cashier to a partner; and from a partner to the head proprietor of the first banking-house in Paris. He became a deputy, and then president of the Council of Ministers. What a destiny for the man who would stoop to pick up a pin!

In the zenith of his prosperity, Lafitte retained the same principles of frugality and saving. He was never the avaricious and grasping miser, but he was ever the parsimonious saver. He would scold, and sometimes read his clerks a lecture upon their wilful waste of a pen, a piece of paper, or an inch of twine; yet he had a heart of charity, and could be munificent in his benevolence. One morning a sister of St. Vincent de Paul entered the bourdoir of the banker, to solicit his subscription to some charitable object. He appeared somewhat ruffled in his temper, but he received her graciously. "What do you require, my good sister," he asked. "Sir," she replied, "I come to you on behalf of my poor neighbours; their distress is great." "Indeed! you have called at the right time, for just now I am angry with that gentleman for wasting my wafers." At the same time, he pointed to a young man seated at a desk, who smiled, but was evidently disconcerted. The sister of charity feared her mission would be a fruitless one; and that her visit might not be without some good result, she amiably applied herself to excuse the fault of the young clerk, who had merited the reproof of the careful money dealer, by not making one wafer serve to seal two letters. Lafitte listened attentively, and afterwards presented to the good sister a check for one thousand francs, saying, at the same time, "If, in my career, I had not economized in trifles, it would not be so easily for me to have contributed to-day to the excellent object which you have in view. Pray look in upon me from time to time!" The character of the banker loses nothing by this regard for little things.

Some years ago, a large dust contractor had a daughter, who was about to be married. His future son-in-law was respectable, but not wealthy, and the match in point of pecuniary circumstances was in his favour. He did not ask for a dowry, but the father of the young lady promised to make them a present on their wedding day. The guests were assembled, the ceremony had been completed, and the father called his son on one side. "I promised to make you a present on your marriage; you observe," said he, pointing through the window at which they were standing, "that large heap of dust, I give it you as my daughter's dowry." The young man bowed, he had expected a few hundred guineas; but he felt chagrined, and almost insulted at such a present. "A heap of dust and dirt, the scrapings of the public street! A fine marriage gift," he murmured to himself, "and a vexatious disappointment!" Nothing more was said at the time; but after the honeymoon he began to think of the dowry. He offered it for sale, and great was his surprise to find the heap of dust, which he had thought so worthless, produce him two thousand pounds. Thus it is, that what some men despise, the frugal and the parsimonious will make the groundwork of a fortune.

There is nothing without its use, and nothing that will not produce a price. Thousands of pounds are earned in London every year, by collecting fragments of old rags, pieces of old nails, and remnants of old cord and twine. These are hoarded up, sorted out, and sold to the proprietors of those dingy receptacles of filth and fat, which are to be found in all the back streets of the metropolis. The "marine store" trade is one of the most profitable in London; by encouraging thrift in others, the dealers in such things grow thrifty themselves.

They learn by their business the value of little things; they will buy a farthing's worth of iron, and a pennyworth of dirty rags. In London, there are a number of amphibious kind of human beings—in appearance neither men nor women, but something between the two. They are known by their peculiar and grotesque appearance. Some wear a hat, but cover their shoulders with a gown. Some are adorned in an old bonnet, but as if to keep up the mystery, button a shabby dress coat tightly round their person. In fact, few could venture to predict to which sex they belong. They are draggled-tailed looking creatures, and some are not unlike the hags in Macbeth. They keep their eyes constantly on the ground, glancing along the gutters of the street with amazing rapidity; and, considering how old they are, it is surprising how quickly they discern the objects of their search. They usually carry a coarse dirty bag, into which they put promiscuously every little bit of linen or woollen rag, string, bone, or iron, which they may be fortunate enough to discover in the mud. The little heaps of dust, swept out by shopboys from behind the counters, are constant mines of treasure, they are sure to find among them something to reward their pains. These singular "snappers up of trifles" are a terror and a mystery to every schoolboy, and they often form the subject of conversation among the junior classes. Many are the traditions current in such places about these mysterious beings. It is said, that a boy, observing one of these thrifty souls busy gathering up something in the streets, and, dying to learn the wonders of her craft, made a sudden snatch at her bag, when out tumbled filth and refuse of all description; dirty rags; bones too stale for even dogs to pick; an old shoe; a dead cat; a part of an iron hoop; sundry lumps of fat; shreds of cloth; horse shoe nails; bits of hempen cord; fragments of coal; pieces of wood, and a catalogue of sundry articles too numerous to mention. Yet these things, thrown away as useless, and thus gathered up, have their value; and many are known to obtain their livelihood in London by these morning gleanings. An old woman, an eccentric character, who may be seen almost every morning rambling about the squares, north of Holborn, is said to have amassed a considerable sum of money in this way; true is it, that one-half of the world knows not how the other half lives.

One October evening, a few years ago, a dirty, ragged, miserable looking, little old man, entered the shop of Mr. James, a broker, in High Street, Gravesend. He wished to know if Mr. James had any objection to receive him as a lodger. He had lived, he said, for many years in Crown Court— certainly not one of the most cheerful, nor respectable localities of the town. His request was complied with, and he took immediate possession of his room, expressing himself much pleased with the accommodation. A short time after he had retired to rest, he was taken ill. The symptoms assumed a serious aspect, and two medical men were sent for. Upon their arrival, Mr. James was informed that his lodger was dying—nothing could save the old man—his end was inevitable; they communicated this sad news quietly to the patient, who immediately ordered an attorney to be sent for. Those around his bed were surprised, for the old man certainly did not look as if he had anything to leave. The attorney, however, was speedily in attendance, the old man raised himself in the bed. "I bequeath," said he, "to my daughter one hundred and fifty pounds, and forty pounds to each of my nephews." The attorney inquired if he had a wife. "No," replied he, "but I have two brothers, and another daughter, who have all behaved very ill towards me; and I shall leave them nothing." When asked to whom he would leave the residue of his property, should there be any; he replied, to Mr. James as a return for his kindness and humanity. At the same time he handed to the attorney a paper parcel, which, on opening, proved to contain securities for upwards of eight hundred pounds in the Bank of England. He died the next morning. It was fortunate for Mr. James that he did not despise the dirty and shabby looking old man. He had received him kindly, and his politeness won for him five hundred sovereigns, which was the amount remaining after all the legacies were paid. This singular character, who was seventy-five years of age at his death, had gathered together much of his money by collecting bits of bone and rag, which he had often been seen to pick up in the streets, and put into his pocket.

CHAPTER III

TRADITIONARY RECOLLECTIONS OF JOHN OVERS, THE SOUTHWARK MISER.

John Overs, the Ferryman—His reputed Parsimony and Avarice—The Miser's Pretty Daughter—Romantic Tale of her Love Adventures—Black Puddings and provender for the Kitchen—His stratagem to save a Meal—He feigns Death; his Servants' rejoicings thereupon—Its Fatal Results—His Burial—Mary Overs and her Lover—Her Misfortunes—Her Retirement from the World, and her Foundation of St. Mary Overs, Southwark.

TRADITIONARY RECOLLECTIONS OF JOHN OVERS, THE SOUTHWARK MISER.

John Overs was a miser, living in the old days when Popery flourished, and friars abounded in England. Some of his vices and eccentricities have been chronicled in a little tract of great rarity, entitled "The True History of the Life and Death of John Overs, and of his Daughter Mary, who caused the Church of St. Mary Overs to be Built." But in giving the particulars of his life, we do not vouch for their authenticity: the tract resembles too strongly a chap book to bear the marks of honest truth; yet the anecdotes are amusing, and the tradition of the miser's pretty daughter reads somewhat romantic.

John Overs was a Southwark ferryman, and he obtained, by paying an annual sum to the city authorities, a monopoly in the trade of conveying passengers across the river. He soon grew rich, and became the master of numerous servants and apprentices. From his first increase of wealth, he put his money out to use on such profitable terms, that he rapidly amassed a fortune almost equal to that of the first nobleman in the land; yet, notwithstanding this speedy accumulation of wealth, in his habits, housekeeping, and expenses, he bore the appearance of the most abject poverty, and was so eager after gain, that even in his old age, and when his body had become weak by unnecessary deprivations, he would labour incessantly, and allow himself no rest or repose. This most miserly wretch, it is said, had a daughter, remarkable both for her piety and beauty; the old man, in spite of his parsimonious habits, retained some affection for his child, and bestowed upon her a somewhat liberal education.

Mary Overs had no sympathy with the avarice and selfishness of her parent: she grew up endowed with amiability, and with a true maiden's heart to love. As she approached womanhood, her dazzling charms attracted numerous suiters; but the miser refused all matrimonial offers, and even declined to negotiate the matter on any terms, although some of wealth and rank were willing to wed with the ferryman's daughter. Mary was kept a close prisoner, and forbidden to bestow her smiles upon any of her admirers, nor were any allowed to speak with her; but love and nature will conquer bolts and bars, as well as fear; and one of her suitors took the opportunity, whilst the miser was busy picking up his penny fares, to get admitted to her company. The first interview pleased well; another was granted and arranged, which pleased still better; and a third ended in a mutual plighting of their troths. During all these transactions at home, the silly old ferryman was still busy with his avocation, not dreaming but that things were as secure on land, as they were on water.

John Overs was of a disposition so wretched and miserly, that he even begrudged his servants their necessary food. He used to buy black puddings, which were then sold in London at a penny a yard; and whenever he gave them their allowance, he used to say, "There, you hungry dogs, you will undo me with eating." He would scarcely allow a neighbour to obtain a light from his candle, lest he should in some way impoverish him by taking some of its light. He used to go to market to search for bargains: he bought the siftings of the coarsest meal, looked out eagerly for marrow-bones that could be purchased for a trifle, and scrupled not to convert them into soup if they were mouldy. He bought the stalest bread, and he used to cut it into slices, "that, taking the air, it might become the harder to be eaten." Sometimes he would buy meat so tainted, that even his dog would refuse it; upon which occasions, he used to say that it was a dainty cur, and better fed than taught, and then eat it himself. He needed no cats, for all the rats and mice voluntarily left his house, as nothing was cast aside from which they could obtain a picking.

It is said that this sordid old man resorted, one day, to a most singular stratagem, for the purpose of saving a day's provision in his establishment. He counterfeited illness, and pretended to die; he compelled his daughter to assist in the deception, much against her inclination. Overs imagined, that like good Catholics, his servants would not be so unnatural as to partake of food whilst his body was above ground, but would lament his loss, and observe a rigid fast; when the day was over, he intended to feign a sudden recovery. He was laid out as dead, and wrapt in a sheet; a candle was placed at his head, in accordance with the Popish custom of the age. His apprentices were informed of their master's death; but, instead of manifesting grief, they gave vent to the most unbounded joy; hoping, at last, to be released from their hard and penurious servitude. They hastened to satisfy themselves of the truth of this joyful news, and seeing him laid out as dead, could not even restrain their feelings in the presence of death, but actually danced and skipped around the corpse; tears or lamentations they had none; and as to fasting, an empty belly admits of no delay. In the ebullition of their joy, one ran into the kitchen, and breaking open the cupboard, brought out the bread; another ran for the cheese, and brought it forth in triumph; and a third drew a flagon of ale. They all sat down in high glee, congratulating and rejoicing among themselves, at having been so unexpectedly released from their bonds of servitude. Hard as it was, the bread rapidly disappeared; they indulged in huge slices of cheese, even ventured to cast aside the parings, and to take copious draughts of the miser's ale. The old man lay all this time struck with horror at this awful prodigality, and enraged at their mutinous disrespect: flesh and blood—at least, the flesh and blood of a miser— could endure it no longer; and starting up he caught hold of the funeral taper, determined to chastise them for their waste. One of them seeing the old man struggling in his sheet, and thinking it was the devil or a ghost, and becoming alarmed, caught hold of the butt end of a broken oar, and at one blow struck out his brains! "Thus," says the tradition, "he who thought only to counterfeit death, occasioned it in earnest; and the law acquitted the fellow of the act, as he was the prime cause of his own death." The daughter's lover, hearing of the death of old Overs, hastened up to London with all possible speed; but riding fast, his horse unfortunately threw him, just as he was entering the city, and broke his neck. This, with her father's death, had such an effect on the spirits of Mary Overs, that she was almost frantic, and being troubled with a numerous train of suitors, she resolved to retire into a nunnery, and to devote the whole of her wealth, which was enormous, to purposes of charity and religion. She laid the foundation of "a famous church, which at her own charge was finished, and by her dedicated to the Virgin Mary." This, tradition says, was the origin of St. Mary Overs, Southwark, a name which it received in memory of its beautiful, but unfortunate foundress.

On an old sepulchre, in St. Saviour's church, may be seen to this day, reclining in no very easy posture, the figure of a poor, emaciated, looking being; which rumour has declared to be the figure of John Overs, the ferryman. There is not much to warrant the conclusion, except, perhaps, the similarity which the mind might discover in the stone effigy; and the aspect with which, in idea, we instinctively endow all such objects of penury. The figure looks thin enough for a man who lived on the pickings of stale bones, and musty bread, it must be allowed; and the countenance certainly looks miserly enough for any miser; but then the marble tablet above merely tells the passer by, that the body of one William Emerson lyeth there, "who departed out of this life," one day in June, in the year 1575.

The curious little tract, from which we have gleaned many of the above particulars, gives a very different account of the miser's burying-place. On account, it is said, of his usury, extortion, and the general sordidness of his life, he had been excommunicated, and refused Christian burial; but the daughter, by large sums of money, endeavoured to bribe the friars of Bermondsey Abbey, to get him buried. As my lord abbot happened to be away from home, the holy brothers took the money, and buried him within the cloister. The abbot on his return seeing a new grave, inquired who, in his absence, had been buried there; and on being informed, he ordered it to be immediately disinterred, and be laid on the back of an ass; then muttering some benediction, or, perhaps, an anathema, he turned the beast from the abbey gates. "The ass went with a solemn pace, unguided by any, through Kent Street, till it came to St. Thomas-a-Watering, which was then the common execution place; and then shook him off, just under the gallows, where a grave was instantly made, and, without any ceremony he was tumbled in, and covered with earth."

CHAPTER IV

SOME ACCOUNT OF THE "GREAT" AUDLEY.

"The Way to be Rich"—A curious Biography of a Miser in the Days of the Commonwealth—Large Savings from Little Earnings—The Cunning of Avarice—A Warning to Drowning Men not to catch at Straws—An Usurer's Schemes and Plots—Fast Young Men of the Commonwealth— The Hypocrisy of Avarice.

SOME ACCOUNT OF THE "GREAT" AUDLEY.

Audley was a celebrated miser of the time of the Stewarts; he amassed his wealth during the reign of the first Charles, and flourished amazingly under the protectorate of Cromwell. His life is displayed by an unknown author, in a tract quaintly entitled the "Way to be Rich, according to the practice of the Great Audley, who began with two hundred pounds in the year 1605, and died worth four hundred thousand pounds this instant, November, 1662." The volume is scarce; and like many scarce volumes, is very insipid in style, and very prosy in detail; but we have thought it worth while to briefly sketch his habits, and thrifty schemes. Audley was originally a clerk, with only six shillings a week salary, and yet out of this scanty sum he managed to save more than half. His dinner seldom cost him anything, for he generally made some excuse to dine with his master's clients; and as to his other meals, a crust of bread or a dry biscuit, was regarded as fare sufficient after an ample dinner. In one circumstance he was somewhat different from other misers; he was clean, if not neat in his outward appearance, but he was thus scrupulous in his apparel from principle; for Audley often asserted, that to be thrifty it was necessary to pay some respect to such matters. He was remarkably industrious, even when a young man. At an age when others were seeking pleasure, he was busy in lending out, and increasing his early savings. He was always ready to work when the usual hours of business were over, and would willingly sit up the whole night to obtain some trifling remuneration. He was never above soliciting trifles, and touching his hat to his master's clients. So rigid was he in his economy, and so usurious in his dealings, that in four years, during which time however he had never received more than a salary of six or eight shillings a week, he managed to save and amass five hundred pounds. The salary of the remaining years of his apprenticeship he sold for sixty, and after awhile, having made up six hundred pounds in all, he lent the whole to a nobleman for an annuity of ninety-six pounds for nineteen years, which annuity was secured upon property producing eight hundred a year. The nobleman soon died, and his heir neglected to pay the annuity. Audley had execution upon the property, and by legal trickery, in which he was well versed, he managed to obtain, in the way of fines and forfeitures, about four thousand pounds profit upon his original six hundred.

His master being one of the clerks of the Compter, Audley had many opportunities of practising his disreputable cunning; and of obtaining vast sums by deluding insolvent debtors, and in deceiving their creditors. He would buy bad debts for a mere trifle, and afterwards compound with the poor insolvent. One instance of his avarice and villainy is so curious, that we cannot refrain from giving the anecdote to our readers. A tradesman named Miller unfortunately got into arrears with his merchant, whose name was White. Many fruitless applications were made for the debt, and at last Miller was sued by the merchant for the sum of two hundred pounds. He was unable to meet the demand, and was declared insolvent. Audley goes to White, and offers him forty pounds for the debt, which the merchant gladly accepts. He then goes to Miller, and undertakes to obtain his quittance of the debt for fifty pounds, upon condition that he entered into a bond to pay for the accommodation. The drowning man catches at a straw, and the insolvent, with many protestations of thanks, eagerly signs a contract which, without consideration, he regarded as one so light, and so easy, in its terms, as to satisfy him that the promptings of benevolence, and friendship, could alone actuate his voluntary benefactor. The contract was, that he should pay to Audley some time within twenty years from that time, one penny progressively doubled, on the first day of twenty consecutive months; and in case he failed to fulfil these easy terms, he was to pay a fine of five hundred pounds. Thus acquitted of his debt of two hundred pounds, Miller arranged with the rest of his creditors, and again commenced business. Fortune turned, and he participated liberally in her smiles. Every month added largely to his trade, and at last he became firmly established. Two or three years after signing the almost forgotten contract, Miller was accosted one fine morning in October by old Audley, who politely demanded the first instalment of the agreement. With a smile, and many renewed expressions of thankfulness, the hopeful tradesman paid his penny. On the first of the succeeding month Audley again called, and demanded twopence, and was as politely satisfied as before. On the first of December, he received a groat; the first of February, one shilling and four pence. Still Miller did not see through the artifice, but paid him with a gracious smile; perhaps, however, there was something cynical in the look of Audley as he left the shop this time, for the poor tradesman's suspicions were aroused, and he put his pen to paper, as he ought to have done years before, to ascertain the amount of his subsequent payments. Reader, what think you would have been the amount of the payment due on the first of the twentieth month? What sum, think ye, the little penny had become? No less than two thousand one hundred and eighty pounds! And what was the aggregate amount of all these twenty monthly payments? Why, the enormous sum of four thousand three hundred and sixty-six pounds, eleven shillings, and three pence! It sounds incredulous, but if you think it a fable, do as Miller did, and reckon for yourselves. Of course Miller refused the payment of his bond, and forfeited five hundred pounds by the benevolence and charity of the miser.

Such is a single instance of the cunning of avarice as displayed, on many occasions, by this miser. His whole life was one of trickery and disreputable craft. His schemes of villainy were so intricate, and his deceptions so subtle, that few could discover their purpose, or tread the labyrinth of his plot. By means of a set of clerks, as disreputable as himself, he became known to the gay gallants of the day as a professed money-lender. "Nor were," says his anonymous biographer, "the youngsters so needy; as Audley was ready to feed them with money, sometimes with a covetous violence forcing upon them more than they desired." Of course always providing that the security was substantial, and the "consideration" dazzling. Of all the lawyers who disgraced their profession, there was never one so disreputable as Audley—there was never usurer so usurious—never a creditor so unrelenting; and there never was one whose craft wrought the ruin of so many unfortunate, but honest men. As the cunning spider before he crawls from his hiding-place to pounce upon his hapless prey, allows it to attempt an escape, that it may be exhausted by fruitless struggles, and become entwined more securely within the snare; lest the sudden appearance of his own ugly self should terrify his victim into some burst of momentary violence, by which he would rend the frail fabric of his net, and escape the flimsy designs of his destroyer. So, did this wretch of avarice, entice the extravagant into acts of still greater profligacy, that he might secure them more entirely within his meshes, before he allowed them to fathom his dastardly schemes of ruin, and his plans of deep and accomplished villany. He would secure himself by bonds and mortgages on magnificent estates, and would do all he could to encourage the thoughtless borrower in a vicious course of life. He never refused to "advance," and was always ready to proffer his advice.

The "fast" young gentlemen of the day, who wore high boots, slouched hats, and gaudy swords, thought him "a good sort of fellow," for he had always money to gratify their desires, and to keep up the game. It is often the case, that they who glory in having "seen the world," and who seem to imagine that they have gained much, by peeping beneath the veil of vice, are the most easily deceived; and, instead of becoming wise by their experience, remain the merest simpletons on earth, to be fleeced by every knave, with a common share of cunning, and to be deceived by the smooth-tongued hypocrisy of every villain, who will call himself their friend. Thus it was, that old Audley found his gay customers obsequious in their obedience to his wishes, and always thankful for his advice. He generally advised his debtors to sell, before they borrowed too much, the straggling parts of their estates; assuring them that they would scarcely be sensible of such sales. "These he would buy of them at half their value; so that the feathers would buy the goose, and the wood pay for the ground; and when the poor gentleman had, with his money, stopped one gap, by prodigality he would open another. O! how the principal, the use, the compound interest, swell the debt, to an incredible sum, until half the estate was sold; and then the old man knew that when half the estate was gone, the gentleman would live as if he enjoyed the whole, and though he abated his possessions, he abated not in expenses; how subtilely would he let his debts grow on, until they became a considerable sum. Gentlemen could not be more careless to pay, than he was willing to continue the debt, knowing that, Bonds, like infants, battle best with sleeping."

This old sinner was a great hypocrite, and, with all his villainy, made some outward show of piety. "He took care," says his biographer, "to accompany himself, to his dying day, with some grave and reverend divine, from whom, if he gained not piety, he gained the reputation of it. He would have, in his chamber, upon the table, a large bible, and Bishop Andrews' Sermons; and if you surprised him not, you might find him busie with one of these books, but if you came suddenly, he was in his closet."

CHAPTER V

MISERS—THEIR HABITS, SCHEMES, AND VICES.

Turner, a Miser, mentioned by Pope—Sir James Lowther and the suspicious halfpenny—A Warning to the Avaricious, in the horrible Death of Foscue, the Miser—Richard Child, the Miser of Colsall—Illustrations of Acquisitiveness, and the love of Hoarding—John Little, the Miser, of Kentish Town—Anecdote of Sir Thomas Colby—Life and Death of Vandille, the Miser of Paris—The rich Sir William Smyth, and Taylor the Oculist—A Miser starved by his own Parsimony—John Mounsey, of Patrickdale—Difficulties of making a Will—Better go to Prison than not save, or Anecdotes of Ben Pope, the Miser—Dick Jarret, the Miser, of Rye—Augustine Partheny, the Dublin Miser; his singular Scheme to save, after Death—Clerical Avarice, or the reverend Miser of Blewbury—How to Repair Old Garments, and make Two Ends meet.

MISERS—THEIR HABITS, SCHEMES, AND VICES.

Facts are more conclusive than conjecture, and to enable our readers to behold the manifestations of avarice, we have thrown together, in our present chapter, an accumulation of anecdotes, which may amuse, by their eccentricity, and prove instructive, as illustrations of the workings of the human mind.

Pope, in his 'Moral Essays,' speaks of a miser, of the name of Turner, who was worth upwards of three hundred thousand pounds. The interest on money being reduced from five to four per cent., he immediately put down his coach, and, discontented with the reduced interest, he put out seventy thousand pounds to a charitable corporation, at an advanced rate. The institution failed, and the miser lost his money, which he took so much to heart, that he kept his chamber ever afterwards, quite broken down in spirits. His grief, at this diminution of his fortune, was so intense, that it was thought he would have sunk under it; but he was heir to a vast estate, and, in expectation of this fortune, he resorted to the plan of keeping to his bedchamber, to save his clothes, and other ordinary expences. Dr. King relates an anecdote of Sir James Lowther, which exemplifies the meanness of avarice. One day he went into George's Coffee House, and ordered a dish of coffee; on leaving, he offered a piece of silver in payment, from which the waiter took twopence, and gave the knight the change in coppers. He was then helped into his chariot, for he was very old and infirm, and drove away. Some days after, he returned to the same coffee house, to acquaint the woman who kept it, that she had given him a bad halfpenny, and to demand another in exchange for it. Sir James had about thirty thousand pounds per annum, and was at a loss whom to appoint his heir.

In the year 1762, an extraordinary instance of avarice occurred in France. A miser, of the name of Foscue, who had amassed enormous wealth, by the most sordid parsimony, and the most discreditable extortion, was requested, by the Government, to advance a sum of money, as a loan. The miser, to whom a fair interest was not inducement sufficiently strong, to enable him to part with his treasured gold, declared his incapacity to meet this demand; he pleaded severe losses, and the utmost poverty. Fearing, however, that some of his neighbours, among whom he was very unpopular, would report his immense wealth to the Government, he applied his ingenuity to discover some effectual way of hiding his gold, should they attempt to institute a search to ascertain the truth or falsehood of his plea. "With great care and secrecy, he dug a deep cave in his cellar; to this receptacle for his treasure he descended by a ladder, and to the trap door he attached a spring lock, so that, on shutting, it would fasten of itself. By and bye the miser disappeared; inquiries were made; tho house was searched; woods were explored, and the ponds were dragged; but no Foscue could they find; and gossips began to conclude that the miser had fled, with his gold, to some part, where, by living incognito, he would be free from the demands of the Government. Some time passed on; the house in which he had lived was sold, and workmen were busily employed in its repair. In the progress of their work they met with the door of the secret cave, with the key in the lock, outside. They threw back the door and descended with a light. The first object upon which the lamp was reflected, was the ghastly body of Foscue the miser, and scattered around him were heavy bags of gold, and ponderous chests of untold treasure; a candlestick lay beside him on the floor. This worshipper of mammon had gone into his cave, to pay his devoirs to his golden god, and became a sacrifice to his devotion! What must have been the sensations of that miserable man—what the horrors of his situation, when he heard the door close after him, and the spring lock effectually imprison him within his secret mine! How bitter must have been the last struggles of that avaricious soul! How terrible must have been the appeals of conscience within that sordid sinner! How each bag must have disgorged its treasure, and each piece of gold have danced, in imagination, around him as a demon! How hated, when the gnawing pangs of starvation came slowly upon him, must have been that yellow vision; his very heart must have grown sick, at that, which he once so dearly loved! Gold in bags; gold in chests; gold piled in heaps; gold for a pillow; gold strewed upon the ground for him to lie upon! Whilst his taper lasted, turn where he would his eyes, nothing met them but his gold. But when the last flicker died away, and the miser was left in darkness, to dwell upon his coming death, and upon his many sins, how awful must have been the agonies of conscience! How, surely, amidst the gloom of that sepulchre of gold, must the poor whom he had oppressed, and the unfortunate whom he had ruined by his avarice, have rose up to reproach him; and, when the mind became fevered by its last deadly struggles, how the faces of haggard poverty, of hate, and loathing for the miser, must, in one loud, discordant chorus, have cried for vengeance and retribution upon his guilty soul!

Avarice will sometimes defeat its own aim, and guilt has often brought its own punishment. Richard Child, the miser of Colsall, who died in 1772, laid up during the severe dearth which occurred in the year 1739, upwards of a hundred quarters of wheat which he might then have sold, at nineteen pounds the load. He would not take less than twenty; and rather than abate his price he stowed the whole of it away, thinking that the scarcity would increase, and people gladly accede to his demand. The miser was disappointed; and for three and thirty years he had the satisfaction of keeping his corn, and grumbling over his mistake. When he died, the store was brought out of the granary. On inspection it was found so damaged by vermin and time, that only seventeen, out of upwards of one hundred quarters, were at all fit for use; and these were sold at Uxbridge market for eleven guineas the load. But had the miser lived still longer, he would rather have let his corn decay than have sold it at a loss, or have distributed it in purposes of charity.

The love of hoarding was curiously exemplified in the life of John Little, the miser of Kentish Town, who died in 1798, having reached his eighty-fourth year. He was not only a miser but a lumberer of useless trash. He gratified his mania to acquire, without regarding the utility or intrinsic value of the things which he amassed; and we can discover no motive in his accumulations but the mere gratification of the promptings of acquisitiveness. After his death, one hundred and seventy-three pairs of breeches, besides a numerous collection of other antiquated and useless articles of wearing apparel were found in a room which had been kept locked for many years. One hundred and eighty musty old wigs, of all shapes and sizes, yellow, black, and grey, were found stowed away in the coach-house; these he had been many years collecting, and some were left to him as legacies by his friends. So great was Little's antipathy to the married state, which he regarded as totally opposed to all thrifty measures, that he discarded his brother, his only relative, because he had ventured to take unto himself a wife: so violent was his resentment at this extravagant act, that he never afterwards spoke to him. His avarice overwhelmed all nobler feelings, and it was by his distrust and suspicion of others that he became instrumental in his own death. His physician had ordered him to drink a glass of wine occasionally; the miser refused for a length of time to accede to this most extravagant remedy—not that it would require any immediate expenditure of cash, for his cellars were well stored with hoarded wine—wine which had become luscious in its repose, and priceless from its antiquity. But the thought of separating his store lacerated the very sinews of his heart; and it was not until he was laid on a bed of sickness, and found that his physical strength was sinking fast, that he was induced to comply. But so distrustful was the sordid avarice of his nature, that he feared to entrust his own housekeeper with the key of his wine-cellar; and insisted upon being carried down, when he would take out one bottle, and relock the door. The miser grew worse, yet he still insisted upon following this course: one day being taken from his warm bed into the damp and humid vault, he was seized with a shivering fit, which, terminating in an apoplectic stroke, occasioned his death. Sir Thomas Colby, an avaricious soul, mentioned by Dr. King in his "Anecdotes of his Own Time," met with his death in a somewhat similar manner. He lived at Kensington, and was a commissioner in the Victualling Office. One night feeling indisposed he took some medicine, which had the effect of throwing him into a profuse perspiration; all at once, in the middle of the night, it struck him that he had left the key of the cellar on the table of his sitting room; and apprehensive that his servants might visit his store, and rob him of a bottle of wine, he arose from the bed, went down in the dark to search for the key, found it, and returned to his chamber; never again to pass its threshold but as a corpse. He died intestate, and left more than two hundred thousand pounds in the funds, which was shared among five or six day labourers who were his nearest kinsmen, but whom he had perhaps never seen.

Vandille is one of the most remarkable characters, as a miser, that is to be found among the eccentric biographers of France. His riches were immense, and his avarice and parsimony extreme. If it is a true saying that money begets money, it is also a true saying that riches beget avarice. This abject slave to Mammon, to avoid noise and to discourage visits, hired a miserable garret in one of the most obscure parts of Paris. He paid a poor woman a sous a day to wait upon him. Excepting once a week, his diet was never varied; bread and milk for breakfast; the same for dinner and the same for supper all the week round. On a Sunday he ventured to indulge in a glass of sour wine, and he strove to satisfy the compunctions of conscience by bestowing, in charity, a farthing every Sabbath. This munificence, which incurred an expenditure of one shilling and a penny per annum, he carefully noted down; and just before his death he found, with some degree of regret, that during his life he had disbursed no less than forty-three shillings and fourpence. Forty-three shillings and fourpence! prodigious generosity for the richest man in France! Vandille had been a magistrate at Boulogne, and whilst in that office he partly maintained himself, free of cost, by constituting himself milk-taster general at the market. He would munch his scrap of bread, and wash it down with these gratuitous draughts. By such parsimonious artifices, and a most penurious course of life, he succeeded in amassing an enormous fortune, and was in a position to lend vast sums of money to the French government. When he had occasion to journey from Boulogne to Paris, he avoided the expense of coach-fare by proceeding on foot; and lest he should be robbed, he never carried more than threepence in his pocket, although he had a distance of a hundred and thirty miles before him. If he found this sum insufficient, he would profess poverty, and beg from the passengers on the road a trifle to help him on.

In the year 1735, Vandille, the miser, was worth nearly eight hundred thousand pounds! He used to boast that this vast accumulation sprang from a single shilling. He had increased it, step by step, farthing by farthing, shilling by shilling, and pound by pound, from the age of sixteen to the age of seventy-two. For six and fifty years had that covetous old man lived, for no other purpose than to accumulate gold which he had not the courage to enjoy. Not once during those years had he indulged himself in any luxury, or participated in any pleasure; his life was one continuous sacrifice to mammon. The blessings which a kind and benevolent providence has bestowed in his mercy upon mankind, were never accepted by Vandille; his whole soul was absorbed; his every joy was sought for in the yellow heap, which his avarice had accumulated. His death was a singular one; the end of that man was a terrible lesson, and one from which a fearful moral may be drawn. The winter of the year 1734, had been very cold and bitter, and the miser felt inclined to purchase a little extra fuel in the summer time, to provide, to some extent, against the like severity in the ensuing winter. He heard a man pass the street with wood to sell; he haggled for an unconscionable time about the price, and at last completed his bargain, at the lowest possible rate. Avarice had made the miser dishonest, and he stole from the poor woodman several logs. In his eagerness to carry them away, and hide his ill-gotten store, he overheated his blood, and produced a fever. For the first time in his life he sent for a surgeon. "I wish to be bled," said he; "what is your charge?" "Half a livre," was the reply. The demand was deemed extortionate, and the surgeon was dismissed. He then sent for an apothecary, but he was also considered too high; and he at last sent for a poor barber, who agreed to open the vein for threepence a time. "But friend," said the cautious miser, "how often will it be requisite to bleed me?" "Three times," replied the barber. "Three times!" and pray what quantity of blood do you intend to take from me at each operation?" "About eight ounces each time," was the answer. "Let me see," said the possessor of three-quarters of a million, "that will be ninepence; too much; too much. I have determined to go a cheaper way to work; take the whole twenty-four ounces at once, and that will save me sixpence." The barber remonstrated, but the miser was firm; he was certain, he said, that the barber was only desirous to extort an extra sixpence, and he would not submit to such scandalous imposition. His vein was opened, and four-and-twenty ounces of blood were taken from him. In a few days, Vandille, the miser, was no more. The savings of his life, the wages of his vice and avarice, he left to the king of France.

A similar anecdote is related of Sir William Smyth, of Bedfordshire. He was immensely rich, but most parsimonious and miserly in his habits. At seventy years of age he was entirely deprived of his sight, unable to gloat over his hoarded heaps of gold; this was a terrible affliction. He was persuaded by Taylor, the celebrated oculist, to be couched; who was, by agreement, to have sixty guineas if he restored his patient to any degree of sight. Taylor succeeded in his operation, and Sir William was enabled to read and write without the aid of spectacles, during the rest of his life. But no sooner was his sight restored, than the baronet began to regret that his agreement had been for so large a sum; he felt no joy as others would have felt, but grieved and sighed over the loss of his sixty guineas! His thoughts were now how to cheat the oculist; he pretended that he had only a glimmering, and could see nothing distinctly; for which reason, the bandage on his eyes was continued a month longer than the usual time. Taylor was deceived by these misrepresentations, and agreed to compound the bargain, and accepted twenty guineas instead of sixty. Yet Sir William was an old bachelor, and had no one to care or provide for. At the time Taylor attended him, he had a large estate, an immense sum of money in the stocks, and six thousand pounds in the house.

In the year 1790, there died in the city of Paris, almost from starvation, a miser worth one hundred and twenty-five thousand pounds. Ostervald, the banker, was well known in his day. He was one of the most acute, and one of the most successful stock-jobbers in France. He had practised from early life habits of the most pinching parsimony. Every night he resorted to a tavern, much frequented by the commercial class, and called for a pint of small beer, for which he paid three sous; and never, even in his most lucky days, nor when fortune had been most propitious, did he exceed that expenditure. In his early days he had practised the same habit; he was always observed to look eagerly for stray corks; to pick them up from the floor, or gather them off the table; these he carried home, and hoarded up. In the course of eight years, he had collected so many, that he was enabled to sell them for twelve louis d'ors. This was the foundation of his great fortune, which he accumulated by rigid parsimony, cunning, and fortunate speculation. When on the bed of sickness, and near unto his death, the miser could not conquer the passion of avarice. He was recommended by his doctor to partake of a little soup every day, to revive his exhausted strength; meat seldom passed his lips, and he had for years subsisted on bread and milk, copiously diluted with water. He regarded, therefore, the soup as extravagance, and the persuasions and importunities of friends were unavailing. "It is true," said he, "I should not dislike the soup, but I have no appetite for the meat; what then was to become of that?" In a few days the miser was a corpse. Around his neck was discovered a small bag made of silk, containing assignats to the value of eight hundred thousand livres.

John Mounsey, of Patrickdale, in the parish of Barton, in

Westmorland, was a most remarkable miser, and well deserves a place among our eccentric memoirs. His property was considerable, and the family mansion, on the lake Ulswater, gave dignity and importance to the Mounseys. Avarice in John, however, was innate; and from very early life he gave many manifestations of this ruling passion. Of all his play-fellows he had the largest property in marbles, and the greatest sums invested in buttons—he became the vender of these juvenile species of stock to all his acquaintance—he was the banker of the school-room, and his exchanges were always carried on upon the most sound principles of finance. His marbles, as soon as won, by play, fair or foul, he endeavoured to dispose of, and he gloried in the accumulation of genuine coin, which his acute and sordid mind taught him to value before the baubles of the play-ground. Thus nourished, and thus encouraged in his propensity to acquire, the youth grew up a wretched votary of avarice. All the usual joys of vigorous youth were insipid—all the sports of youthful innocence were distasteful, and all the sanguine hopes, and bright anticipations of opening manhood, were clouded and warped by his anxious and fevered pursuit for wealth. At the death of his father, which occurred when he was a young man, he came in possession of three hundred pounds per annum; but with this new acquisition of revenue his appetite for gold increased, rather than diminished. He would employ himself in the meanest occupations, and in the most laborious labour—he would sleep in a barn to save the cost of a tavern bed, and he presented, in his outward appearance, one of the most miserable objects of wretchedness and filth; indeed, to look upon him was to learn how deplorable and sinful were the consequences of that grovelling lust which guide the actions of the miser, and transform the noble image of man into the semblance of a brute. His coat was patched with pieces of dirty cloth, and his stockings with fragments of refuse leather, which he had been fortunate enough to meet with in his rambles. He wore wooden-shoes, thickly shod with iron, and an old hat without brim or nap; if he had particular business to transact from home, which required a more decent appearance, he borrowed a few clothes of a friend. One day whilst ferrying a load of wood down the lake with his man Pearson, he displayed the fortitude of his avarice. A violent storm arose—the winds blew a hurricane—the rain came down in torrents, and well nigh sunk the boat; and thunder and lightning filled their hearts with terror. The boat was in danger, but to throw their cargo overboard was too great a sacrifice, and an act of waste to which no miser could submit; rather than do so, for two days and two nights he braved the storm; neither danger, nor cold, nor hunger, nor the entreaties of his companion, could persuade him to relieve the boat of its weight. On the third day, the storm abated, and, with the assistance of some peasantry, they landed in safety. Mounsey was so penurious that his whole expenses did not exceed twenty or thirty pounds per annum; although he was proprietor of land which produced him eight hundred pounds per annum. To guard against robbers, he was in the habit of hiding his money in old stone walls; his visits to the place at which he was wont to secret large sums, excited, on one occasion, the suspicions of an old woman, who, when he had left, commenced a diligent search of the wall; stone after stone she loosened and replaced, but no success rewarded her industry. She determined, however, to discover by stratagem what she could not find by labour. When the miser the next day approached the wall, she tumbled a quantity of stones about, and ran off, pretending she had discovered the hidden treasure. The trick was successful, and the alarmed miser ran after her to beg and implore her to return the gold; he even offered her half if she would return the rest. The old woman was now convinced that the money was hid near the place of her recent search; and before the miser could recover from his consternation she returned, and, pulling out a few more stones, discovered a bag of gold, which she carried off in triumph.

A horse was considered too expensive to maintain, although Mounsey was constantly requiring one on his estate. He endeavoured to avoid so much extravagance by joining with a neighbour in the purchase of a nag; the partners, however, soon quarrelled, for when the poor animal was employed by Mounsey, he usually fasted throughout the day. Turnpike gates, too, were always avoided to save the toll, and tedious and circuitous routes added to the fatigues of the day; the horse grew like the rider, and every rib could have been accurately counted. Mounsey always walked with his eyes upon the ground in search of old rags and refuse. One day as he was riding to Penrith Market, by the Banks of Ulswater, he made a sudden stop—got off the back of his redoubtable nag—stripped himself, and walked into the lake to pull out an old dirty stocking, which he had observed through the limpid waters, lying at the bottom of the stream. In one of the last acts of his life, that of making his will, he was equally parsimonious. He bargained with a poor schoolmaster, of the name of Wilson, to write this document for tenpence; but alterations were so frequent that the village pedagogue remonstrated upon the lowness of the price, and the miser munificently offered to raise the sum to a shilling; the scribe, however, demanded half-a-crown, which was deemed so exorbitant that Mounsey employed another person. The dictating of a will is a hard thing for such men as John Mounsey, the allotting and parcelling out of that for which they have sacrificed all social comforts, and all domestic joys; for which they have darkened their lives, and perilled their souls in the world to come, is a hard and bitter task. It is like signing a warrant for one's own death—it is like squeezing blood from a heart of stone—a thing almost as difficult. The miser has found it impossible to part with his gold in life, and now he can scarcely gather up the courage to bequeath it in death. He seems to be relaxing the tenacity of his holding when he consents to devise and bequeath. He groans at every item of the ominous document, and would strive, as it were, to reserve some portion of his wealth for the time when wealth can no longer avail, and when gold can no longer impart delight.

"I give, I devise," old Euclio said
And sigh'd, "My lands and tenements to Ned."
"Your money sir?" "My money, sir! What! all?
"Why if I must (then wept) I give to Paul."
"The manor, sir?" "The manor! Hold!" he cried.
"Not that—I cannot part with that"—and died!

— Pope.

Mounsey's son, who did not inherit the propensity of acquisitiveness from his father, but who retained a generous and noble heart, in spite of his niggardly education, and the pernicious examples and sordid admonitions which his parent had endeavoured to instil into his mind, advised the miser to leave two hundred pounds to the poor. "No," he said; "he had lost a great deal by the poor, but he never got anything from them in his life. Why, therefore, should he leave anything to them?" The son remonstrated with his dying father, and spoke of his duty as a Christian. "Well," said he at last to his only son, who was his sole heir and executor, "I will leave one hundred pounds, if you will pay fifty!" Thus, with death before him, did the habits of the miser appear. He died on the 15th of October, 1793, after a long life of two and ninety years. His last words were words of regret that he could not live longer to grow richer!

Social comforts are willingly sacrificed, and corporeal

deprivations are cheerfully borne, by the miser, if the sacrifice and deprivation tend to advance the great object of his life, and help to gratify his propensity to save. It is more easy for the miser to endure imprisonment than to part with his gold. Old Ben Pope, the miser, of Southward, who was supposed to be worth seventy thousand pounds, was fined for some nefarious money transactions with Sir Alexander Leith—ten thousand pounds by way of damages. To evade the fine, Benjamin went to France, but afterwards returned to England, and resolved to show his resentment by going into the Fleet. For eleven years and three months he suffered imprisonment with philosophy and patience. At one time, his creditor was willing to compound, and tendered him his liberty for a thousand pounds; but Pope refused even this offer: he would rather die, he told them, than submit to such extortion. He carried, during his imprisonment, his habits of parsimony to the utmost extreme, seldom partaking of anything superior to a hard crust and an atom of the rind of cheese. A joint of meat was never known to have graced his table. On one memorable occasion, it was remarked that he indulged himself in a fourpenny plate of meat from the cookshop; but the indulgence was never afterwards repeated. Water was his usual beverage; but every other day, to sustain what little strength he had, he purchased a pint of beer, never omitting, before he paid for it, to examine well the measure, to ascertain that it was full: if, when the froth had disappeared, the liquor was not level with the brim, he would storm and haggle for an hour. He used to purchase a three farthing candle, but he would not complete his purchase unless the vendor would allow him to choose one himself from the box; and he used to chuckle to himself, when he was so fortunate as to find one a little thicker than the rest. After a life of sixty-seven years, the greatest portion of which had been spent in penury and misery like this, he died in prison worth seventy thousand pounds. The old inhabitants of Rye still remember Dick Jarret, the miser. He was one of those greedy and covetous souls that would scruple to take two sixpences for a shilling, lest by any chance he should lose by the exchange. He lived by himself: he never had the heart to love, nor the courage to marry. His diet was of the poorest and most comfortless description; and he grumbled in his old age at the hardness of the times, complaining that formerly his expenditure never exceeded six pounds per annum, but that latterly, on account of the dearness of provision, his household and other expences had cost thirteen pounds per annum. His dress corresponded with these wretched habits: any one could recognise in him the victim of a sordid avarice. At his death, he had in his celler some wine, which had been made for his christening seventy years before, he had never ventured to partake of it during his life, but left it for his relatives to make merry over at his funeral. He died in the year 1806, worth ten thousand pounds: his hoards might, perhaps, have exceeded that amount, for it is doubtful whether his hidden treasures were all discovered at the time—three hundred guineas were found under a brick in the floor, and notes were discovered in unsuspected crevices.

For our next illustration of the passion of avarice, we would refer to the life of Augustine Partheny, the Dublin miser. He was originally a journeyman cooper; but, when a young man, he relinquished his trade, and took a voyage to the West Indies, in company with his maternal uncle. Both uncle and nephew were of a plodding, parsimonious, disposition. The uncle made a fortune, and the nephew returned home with a tolerable share of riches, but with a discontented mind. His acquisitiveness had been excited: the possession of a little only fed the desire for more: he neither used nor enjoyed what he had; still, the promptings of avarice were strong within him, and he again left his country to seek in Antigua and Santa Cruz for fresh accumulations. His voyage was eminently successful, and he again returned home to lock up and to unlock—to count over and to pile up—to admire and to gloat upon his heaps of gold. But although he possessed one of the largest fortunes in Dublin, he was one of the most wretched objects of penury. In his person he was dirty and unprepossessing; and in his temper he was morose and scurrilous. He was never known to have bestowed praise upon others, and no one could ever boast of his friendship. The lust for gold, and the constant worshipping of his wealth, had effectually closed his heart to all human sympathies. He was never known to have shed a tear of sorrow, or to mourn for the death of kindred. He was never known to utter one word of compassion for the afflicted. He was never known to have distributed one mite from his crowded coffers in purposes of charity, and he was never known to have received one grateful look from the eyes of the sick, nor one honest benizen from the lips of poverty. He sought not for the blessings, and he cared not for the curses of the poor. He never entered society, but shunned all intercourse with the world. Of the society of females, he had an utter abhorence: with the true principles of rigid parsimony he looked upon matrimony with affright, and treated all women with contempt. It is probable that the fair sex entertained a similar feeling for the miser; for the longer he lived, the deeper he became rooted in his antipathy to their presence; a result almost impossible, had they exerted their feminine art to flatter his vanity, or to tolerate his company. He retained his love of gold in all its virulence, to the last day of his life; just before his death, a friendly neighbour sent him a physician, which he did not appear to dislike, but suddenly recollecting that, probably, the doctor would demand his fee, he became restless and uncomfortable; he raised himself in the bed, "Doctor," said he, "I am a strong man, and know my disorder, but as Mr. Nangle has sent you to my assistance, I shall not exchange you for any other person, if we can come to terms; in fact, I wish to know your charge for attendance, until I am recovered." The physician answered, "eight guineas." "Ah! sir," exclaimed the old miser, anxious to make a pinching bargain, "if you knew my disorder, you would not be so exorbitant; but to put an end to this discussion, I will give you six guineas and a-half." The doctor assented, and the patient gave the physician the stipulated sum. He died in 1811, after a long life of eighty-six years, but although his relatives were numerous, he did not leave them any part of his enormous wealth, which at his death amounted to three hundred thousand pounds. With the exception of four pounds per annum to his servant, who had been in his employ for four and twenty years, he bequeathed the whole of his fortune to a rich family in the West Indie. It was left, however, upon condition that they were to allow this vast sum to accumulate and improve for fourteen years, before they received it. Thus, not content with saving during his life, he was anxious to save after his death, it was a strange consolation for a dying sinner, that his wealth, the sordid accumulations of his useless life, should go on increasing long after he had himself mouldered into dust.

Who, down at Blewbury, has not heard of the Rev. Mr. Jones, whose rigid habits of parsimony exceeded even those of the celebrated John Elwes. This godly miser was curate of Blewbury for forty-five years. His stipend did not exceed fifty guineas per annum, and yet he died in 1827 worth many thousands of pounds. He was fortunate enough, at the death of a relative, to come into the possession of a little property, which produced him thirty pounds per annum, and which, with his salary, and the interest of his savings for the previous year, he always invested in the funds. Upon the fees of his office, which averaged about half-a-crown a week, he contrived to live; and even from that scanty allowance has been known to extract a saving of a few pence. He kept no servant, and never engaged any one to clean his rooms, or to assist in his domestic concern; he fulfilled himself the duties of the housemaid, chambermaid, and cook, and officiated as his own washerwoman and tailor. In appearance he was a walking scarecrow, and the hat which he had upon his head, and the rags which he had upon his hack, were enough to frighten all the birds in the neighbourhood. The same hat and coat served him during the whole forty-five years that he lived at Blewbury. As specimens of industry, and curious stitching, they were both remarkable articles of wearing apparel. The brim of his hat on his left side was, by dint of constant handling, entirely worn off; one day, on coming from Upton, across the fields, he luckily espied an old hat stuck upon a pole, in a cornfield, to frighten away the birds; he immediately seized the prize and despoiled it of its brim, which he sewed on to his own hat with a piece of twine. It is doubtful, whether the addition was an improvement, for the new brim was a jet black, whilst the old head was of a most dingy brown. As to his coat, it was a miracle of art; if Joseph's coat surpassed it in the variety of its colours, it was nothing to it in the multiplicity of its patches. There never was a coat so twisted and turned, so doctored and repaired, so altered in its fashion, or so metamorphosed in its shape, as the coat of the Rev. Mr. Jones. The life of that coat would have been an entertaining history; it would have taught those who wish to make a surtout, do double duty, how to achieve their end. When he first went to Blewbury, it was then the worse for wear, and after some considerable time, when it had become threadbare, and of the hue of russet, he had it turned inside out, and converted into a dress coat. This napless garment soon became dangerously thin, and subject to incessant rents, and tears, which continually kept its reverend owner employed; it was the practice of this thrifty curate to borrow needle and thread on these occasions of the neighbouring farmers, for to have invested any capital in the purchase of such articles, would have been a serious and weighty consideration. But at last, in spite of all his care and patching, pieces fell out, and were lost; to repair these dilapidations, he cut fragments off the tail, and sewed them in neatly himself. At last, this system of robbing one part to repair another, became so frequent, and the tails were so reduced, that the coat became a jacket, and certainly there never was a garment that so disgraced "the cloth," as that worn by this most reverend miser; old crones used to envy it as a piece of ingenious patchwork, and youthful rustics used to wonder, whether it could be Joseph's coat— grown dingy, and discoloured by time, which the curate would sometimes tell them about in his morning lesson; indeed, so much amazement and consternation did the tailless jacket produce, that Mr. Jones was at last compelled to refrain from appearing in it before the public eye; but he was constantly decorated in this strange garment when at home. In other articles of his apparel the curate was equally parsimonious. He had a great store of new shirts, neatly folded up, and locked within his drawers; but, with the exertion of one solitary shirt, they were never allowed to part company; when he had it washed, which was only once in two or three months, he went about without a shirt at all, rather than take one of the new ones into use. He always took it off at night, that it might last clean the longer; and when it became worn, he always mended it himself, and repaired it on the same plan that he repaired his coat; the consequences were of course the same; the shirt became tailless, and no longer reached down to his knees. Sorely was the reverend miser tempted to disturb his hoarded linen, and to take a new one into use; but after a diligent search, he found in one of his drawers the top of a shirt, with a frill on, which had lain by ever since his gay and youthful days; this, with his usual sagacity, he tacked into the old shirt, with the frill hanging downwards, which embellished that useful garment with a novel and elegant appearance. In his diet Mr. Jones was as singular and as penurious as in his dress. On a Saturday he purchased the food which was to last him during the ensuing week, and he cooked the whole of his provisions on the Sunday. His meals were never varied, and he never purchased but three articles, bread, bacon, and tea, which he used to term two necessaries, and one luxury. This was invariably his diet all the year round; if his bread became dry, or his bacon "cupboardy," it was all the same; he rather, in fact, encouraged within himself a dislike for his meals, because he found it a saving; and it was always his aim to make one week's allowance, if possible, suffice for two; this he would sometimes manage by dining gratuitously with a neighbour. It was remarked, that although he was frequently entertained by his parishioners, only one person during ten years had ever been known to have sat at his table: this was a particular friend, and he only obtained a crust of bread, after much difficulty and importunity. In fact, the larder never contained anything but bread, and a piece of unsavoury bacon; no meat, sugar, coffee, cheese, milk, or such class of common provisions, ever entered his house; yet our parsimonious curate always manifested the utmost pleasure when he could partake of such luxuries free of expense. His common beverage was water, and at breakfast and supper he indulged in a cup of weak tea, unflavoured with milk or sugar. Few liked a glass of ale more than did the Rev. Mr. Jones, and yet he never spent but a single sixpence in that liquor during the whole time that he was curate of Blewbury. The farmers would occasionally, however, treat him to a glass, which formerly he used never to refuse; but being invited to a rustic wedding, about ten years before his death, he drank so freely of strong ale, and made so many grimaces, and played such unaccountable tricks for a parson, that the parishioners talked about it for some days, which so mortified this reverend gentleman, that he made a vow never to indulge in any stronger drink than his diluted tea; a vow which, it is said, he piously and scrupulously observed. Mr. Jones never lit a fire, however cold the weather, except on a Sunday, for the purpose of cooking his bacon, and brewing his tea; this was usually one of sticks and rubbish, which he was often seen busily collecting in the churchyard; he never could persuade himself to use coal, although he had a shed at the back of his house full of that article. On cold winter evenings he would beg a seat by the cheerful fire of a neighbour, and after warming his shivering limbs return, and immediately get to bed, to keep in the heat. It was one night returning thus that the old man died, comfortless, and alone; after having deprived himself of every comfort, and denied himself many of the necessaries of life, that he might leave thousands to relatives whom he had never seen.

CHAPTER VI

NOTICES OF JEMMY TAYLOR THE BOROUGH USURER.

Curious anecdotes of his life—His penurious habits—His tempting cookery—His companions—The Earl of Northumberland and the money-lender—His pleasure in hoarding—His first and only act of charity—His death—Curious epitaph.

NOTICES OF JEMMY TAYLOR THE BOROUGH USURER.

Jemmy Taylor, called by his contemporaries the Southwark miser, was a native of Leicestershire; he was brought up to the trade of a weaver, but he forsook it for the more lucrative one of stockbroker. He was an acute and cunning man, and soon became a successful adept on 'Change. He could fabricate news, spread false reports, excite distrust, or inspire confidence, with an activity and effect which many of his brethren would envy, but few could learn to imitate with similar success. So learned did he become in all the trickery of 'Change, that he grew immensely rich. There is a profound mystery connected with the Stock Exchange; such matters as interest, discount, transfers, debentures, bills, shares, and scrips, are even in the present day plunged in obscurity, to half the people who read for the sake of appearances the city news. This perplexity was considerably greater in the golden days of Jemmy Taylor, and the profits of stockbroking were monopolized by a choice and favoured few. Taylor was one of the most successful, and is said to have amassed a fortune of two hundred thousand pounds, by his money speculations. But this vast sum was accumulated without enjoyment, save the enjoyment derived from the gratification of his acquisitive propensity. He lived in a house which few would condescend to inhabit, and which the most impoverished would look upon with disdain. The wind blew through innumerable crevices in the walls, and whistled through broken panes; the rain spattered down from huge apertures in the roof, and the very stairs creaked with their ancient rottenness. His chamber was in all respects the chamber of a miser; dreary, desolate, and chilly. His bed was a truss of straw, and a few dirty rags served him for sheets; his food was of the most scanty and penurious description, and his clothes would have disgraced the indigent by their ragged filthiness; they were often the means of enabling this thrifty being to add a penny to his store; for the benevolent, thinking him destitute, frequently bestowed upon him some trifle in charity. One day, some ladies near the Bank, supposing him to be in great want, gave him sixpence, which he received with a low bow, and immediately set off to purchase a twopenny steak, which, on returning, he carried in his hand, to show them that he had not misapplied their bounty.

Jemmy Taylor enjoyed the friendship of several who were as avaricious, and as parsimonious, as himself. The famous Daniel Dancer was a great favourite, and was sometimes invited to partake of his hospitality. On one occasion, two bankers' clerks calling upon Taylor, found him busily engaged in boiling one solitary mutton chop in a prodigious quantity of water, to make, what he termed, some comfortable broth for himself and his old friend, Dancer, whom he hourly expected. After some complimentary salutations, the clerks, feeling disposed for fun, induced Jemmy to leave the room, to procure them some refreshment, from a neighbouring tavern; and during his absence they threw into his saucepan three halfpenny candles, which happened to be lying on the table. This was regarded, by the two old misers, as a grateful and savoury acquisition, for they devoured the broth with a relish, and lavishly praised its surpassing richness and strength. The next day Taylor met the two clerks upon 'Change, and accused them of stealing his candles. They declared their innocence, assuring him that they merely committed them to the pot, at the bottom of which, most probably, he would still find the wicks, if they had not, in their hunger, devoured them!

A short time after the American war, it is said, that the Earl of Northumberland having occasion for seventy-four thousand pounds, applied to a broker, who appointed a certain day for the transfer. At the time and place for meeting, there was posted in waiting, old Jemmy Taylor, who, in appearance, resembled some itinerant vendor of matches. Upon the Duke's arrival, the broker brought Jemmy forward to his grace, who, not knowing him, thought he was a beggar, and was about to bestow a trifle upon him, when he was informed that he was "a warm man." His grace immediately shook hands with the dirty usurer, and Jemmy accommodated him with seventy-four thousand pounds, out of one stock, in the four per cents., and from whence, as it appeared by the books, he could have sold out as much more, and yet have had as much left as would have made him comfortable all the rest of his days.

In hoarding up his gold, and denying himself every comfort to do so, Taylor did but follow the promptings of a passion, which, by encouragement, had become inordinate; people with whom he was acquainted, would sometimes endeavour to persuade him of the folly of such penurious habits, and beg of him to indulge in a few of the blessings of life. To all such appeals Taylor turned a deaf ear; and he used to reply, that "if his successors had as much pleasure in spending his property, as he had in hoarding it up, they need not complain of their hard lot in the world!"

A curious anecdote is related of Taylor, in his last days, and as he lay on the bed of sickness. He had little thought of religion, during his career in life, but now, as death approached, he felt some compunctions of conscience. He hoped, by sacrificing a small portion of his ill-gotten store, to absolve his sins, and to purchase some reward hereafter. He sent for the parish officers, the parson, and the curate, and, entreating their prayers, he paid them down twelve hundred pounds; but it is said that he would not conclude his bequest until they consented to return him a twelvemonths' interest, by way of discount for prompt payment!

His name, we believe, still adorns the donation board of Saint Saviour's Church, in the Borough. He died in 1793, and the following curious, but no very flattering Epitaph, was inserted by some wag, in the evening papers of the time: —

HERE LIES JEMMY TAYLOR,

alias

Gripus, the Soutthwark Miser,

Who lived and died single to save Expences.

HIS MATCHLESS OECONOMY

Could only be compared to his singular Resolution in

SELF-DENIAL.

He was so disinterested in his Disposition, that he never

Preferred one Person to another, but cast an equal

Eye upon all his Acquaintance.

His mind was of such a peculiar Cast, that he could neither

Hear the Tale, nor behold the Face of the Wretched;

And to avoid mistaken Acts of Charity,

Never bestowed the smallest Mite upon the Poor, until

Death, that shakes the strongest Head, whispered,

"TAYLOR, give something to the CHURCH."

Envied by the Avaricious for his vast Wealth,

Detested by the malicious World for his severe Virtues,
And regretted by none of his
FRIENDS UPON THE 'CHANGE,
He gave up this Life, with Fears of a Better,
In the Seventieth Year of his Existence;
And has left his Relations perfectly resigned
To the Will of Heaven,
For having withdrawn, in good Time, the
Accumulator of their Fortunes.

CHAPTER VII

LIFE OF THOMAS GUY THE BOOKSELLER.

Life of Thomas Guy, an Illustration of Parsimony without Avarice—His Speculations and Schemes—His Economy and his Liberality—Anecdote of Guy and Hopkins the Miser—Matrimonial Engagements—Mutability of Love—Death of Guy—His Munificence—Last Will and Testament—Conclusion, &c.

LIFE OF THOMAS GUY THE BOOKSELLER.

As an illustration of extreme parsimony without avarice, we present the reader with a brief sketch of the life and eccentric habits of Thomas Guy. This remarkable man, whose charity far exceeded his habits of saving, was the son of a lighterman and coal-merchant in Horsleydown, Southwark.[1] He was born at the commencement of the civil war: of his education and early life but little is known.

In 1660 he was bound apprentice to John Clarke, a bookseller, living in the porch of Mercer's Hall, Cheapside. As soon as his term was expired, he commenced trading for himself, with a capital of two hundred pounds; he carried on business in a house situated between Cornhill and Lombard Street, and his trade was principally in English Bibles. At that time Bibles were so badly and so carelessly printed in England, that almost every page was disfigured by some typographical error. This induced Guy to enter into a speculation to print them in Holland, and to import them into England, by which scheme a more accurate edition could be sold at a price considerably under that of the London Bibles. The University of Oxford, having by charter certain privileges in the printing of Bibles, interfered

---

1. See Highmore's Pietas Londinensis, 8vo. Lond. 1810, for some account of this singular character.

and prevented our enterprising bibliopole from carrying out his design. He then, however, contracted with the University for the privilege of printing them; and for many years he was enabled to amass considerable sums of money by carrying on an extensive trade in Bibles. This laid the foundation for his vast fortune; for being a bachelor, and naturally of a very frugal and saving disposition, his profits were allowed to accumulate. He was most penurious in his domestic arrangements, and the complete suit of his every day apparel would scarcely have fetched eighteen-pence from the most enterprising Israelite. He usually dined upon his shop counter with an old newspaper or dirty proof-sheet for a table doth. His meals were always of the most frugal nature, and he seldom indulged in luxuries. His savings as a bookseller he speedily augmented by purchasing seamen's tickets, during the continental wars in Queen Anne's time, and by large but cautious speculations in South Sea Stock.

Most of our readers are probably familiar with the history of that celebrated "bubble," and are aware how pernicious were its effects at the time upon the operations of legitimate commerce: the pursuit of trade was abandoned—property was sacrificed at a ruinous loss, and visions of a golden future fevered the imaginations of the most unpretending capitalists. Stock rose enormously; and every man who possessed a portion regarded it as the germ of future affluence. By and bye the bubble burst, and thousands were ruined in the terrible crisis. Gay the poet held some of the stock, which the advice of his more cautious friends could not induce him to part with; he deemed it worth twenty thousand pounds, every penny of which was lost. Some few, more careful than the rest, enriched themselves by selling out when the delusion was in its zenith. Thomas Guy was among this number. In the year 1720 he possessed stock to the amount of forty-five thousand five hundred pounds. His suspicions were excited as to its stability as an investment; and when it rose to about three hundred pounds be began to sell out, and continued doing so until it arose to six hundred, when he disposed of the whole of his remaining property in the stock at that rate. It ultimately, however, reached the almost fabulous price of one thousand and fifty pounds per cent! From beginning to end Thomas Guy is said to have made nearly five hundred thousand pounds by the great South Sea bubble! During all this prosperity Guy observed the most rigid parsimony; but he never allowed his love of saving to render him forgetful of his duties as a Christian. Long before this vast acquisition of wealth he paid for the building of three wards on the north side of the outer court of Saint Thomas's Hospital, and for many years he annually gave one hundred pounds towards the funds of that institution. It is somewhat singular to find such munificence in a person of such penurious habits; and the life of Thomas Guy is a striking proof of the wide distinction we ought to draw between parsimony and avarice: the one is not essentially a selfish or sordid propensity, and its observance may sometimes have for its motive a noble ulterior object in view; whilst avarice is a passion purely selfish, and can never sympathize with such virtues as charity or benevolence. Not that we should deem it necessary to carry the principle of saving to the extent which the following anecdote of Guy displays. It is said that one evening he was sitting in his little back parlour meditating over a handful of half lighted embers, confined within the narrow precincts of a brick stove; a farthing candle was on the table at his side, but it was not lit, and the fire afforded no light to dissipate the gloom; he sat there all alone planning some new speculation; congratulating himself on saving a pennyworth of fuel, or else perchance thinking how else he could bestow some thousand guineas in charity: his thoughts, whether on subjects small or great, were interrupted by the announcement of a visitor; he was a shabby, meagre, miserable looking old man;

but compliments were exchanged, and the guest was invited to take a seat; Guy immediately lighted his farthing candle, and desired to know the object of the gentleman's call: the visitor was no other than the celebrated Hopkins, who on account of his avarice and rapacity had obtained the name of Vulture Hopkins. "He lived," says Pope, "worthless, but died worth three hundred thousand pounds, which he would give to no person living, but left it so as not to be inherited till after the second generation." His counsel represented to him how many years it must be before this could take effect, and that his money would only lie at interest all that time. He expressed great joy thereat, and said they would then be as long in spending as he had been in getting it. But the Chancery afterwards set aside the will, and gave it to the heir at law. The reader will probably remember the lines in Pope's Moral Essays—

> "When Hopkins dies a thousand lights attend,
> The wretch that living saved a candle's end."

"I have been told," said Hopkins, as he entered the presence of Thomas Guy, "that you are better versed in the prudent and necessary art of saving, than any man now living, and I now wait upon you for a lesson in frugality, an art in which I used to think I excelled, but I am told by all who know you that you are greatly my superior." "If that is all you are come about," said Guy, "why then we can talk the matter over in the dark;" so saying, he with great deliberation put the extinguisher on his newly lighted farthing candle. Struck with this instance of economy, Hopkins acknowledged the superior abilities of his host, and took his leave imbued with a profound respect for such an adept in the art of saving.

It is singular to observe what trifling events will sometimes act as a pivot upon which the future events of a life will turn. It is to one of these slight rufflings in the stream of life that the public are indebted for the noble institution which still exists as a monument of the munificient charity of the parsimonious Thomas Guy. "He employed," says Highmore, "a female servant whom he agreed to marry. Some days previous to the intended ceremony he ordered the pavement before his door to be mended up to a particular stone, which he marked, and then left his house on business. The servant in his absence looking at the workman, saw a broken stone beyond the mark which they had not repaired, and on pointing to it with that design, they acquainted her that Mr. Guy had not ordered them to go so far. She however directed it to be done, adding, with the security of feeling incidental to her expectation of soon becoming his wife, "Tell him I bade you, and he will not be angry." But she soon learnt how dangerous it is for any one in a dependent situation to exceed the limits of their authority; for her master, on his return, was so enraged at finding that they had exceeded his orders, and put him to an additional expense, that he renounced his matrimonial engagement with his servant, and devoted his ample fortune to public charity.

When he had reached the age of seventy-six, and found himself possessed of a fortune, which might justly be regarded as enormous for the age, Guy commenced his munificent plans of charity. He took of the Governors of St. Thomas's Hospital, a piece of ground opposite to that building, on a lease of nine hundred and ninety-nine years, at an annual rent of thirty pounds per annum. The spot was, at that time, covered with small tenements, which in a few months he had removed. Plans were drawn out—foundations dug with the utmost speed; and he who had been so solicitous to save a farthing candle, had the gratification to behold, before he died, a handsome hospital erected with a portion of his parsimonious savings. Eighteen thousand seven hundred and ninety-three pounds were expended in the erection of Guy's Hospital; and its eccentric founder, who died in 1724, in his eighty-first year, endowed it with two hundred and twenty thousand pounds, the residue of his estate. Other acts of kindness and charity adorn the memory of this singular but most benevolent man. He bequeathed one thousand pounds for the discharging of four debtors within the City of London, and in the counties of Middlesex and Surrey; by this means, some seven or eight hundred were liberated from prison. He bequeathed to Christ's Hospital a perpetual annuity of four hundred pounds, for taking in four children yearly, on the nomination of the Governors. In his life time he founded some almshouses at Tamworth, which borough he represented in Parliament during several sessions; these almshouses he further endowed by his will with a perpetual annuity of one hundred and twenty-five pounds. Nor did this worthy man forget his numerous relatives—many of them were poor, and most of them were in indifferent circumstances—they all, however, had to be grateful for the parsimony which Guy had practised during his life. Not one of them was forgotten; to some he left small annuities for life, and to others considerable sums of money. To most of his sister's children and cousins, who were very numerous, he left a thousand pounds a piece. Among his poor relatives, in various sums, he left life annuities amounting to near nine hundred pounds per annum; and among his younger relations and executors, he distributed nearly seventy-six thousand pounds. It is seldom that the hoardings of parsimony have been in their distribution so guided by the dictates of benevolence. Guy did not, like the miser, save for the senseless and selfish gratification of an ignoble passion. He saved that he might bestow, and he consecrated his profits in trade, and his accumulations by rigid self-denial to the service of the poor, the unfortunate, and the sick—all honour, and all praise, to the memory of the kind and noble-hearted bookseller!

CHAPTER VIII

THE LIFE OF DANIEL DANCER.

His Birth and Estate—His garments and outward appearance—Miss Dancer and her feminine graces—The Miser's Mansion—The finding of a Treasure—The Story of the Mutton Pies—A-Miser's idea of Death—Bob, the Miser's cur—Griffiths and his Master—How to turn a penny—A substitute for a Fire—The advantages of keeping a Snuff-box— The Miser dies without a Shirt—The Treasures of a Dunghill, &c.

THE LIFE OF DANIEL DANCER.

There are few, who, by their habits of parsimony, have gained such notoriety as Daniel Dancer; by nature he was a complete miser, the passion of avarice in him, obscured during the whole of his life every feeling of virtue, and every trace of natural affection.

The life of Dancer is not without its moral; we behold the vice of an inordinate acquisitiveness in its darkest hues, and we learn how incompetent is wealth to bestow happiness without the presence of virtue and benevolence to guide the mind in its distribution, and to make its accumulation in the hands of one, a blessing to the hearts of many.

Daniel Dancer was born in the year 1716, he was the oldest of a family of three boys, and one girl; his father lived on Harrow Weald Common, on Harrow-on-the-Hill, where he possessed property, which produced a comfortable income; we have no information relative to the habits and character of the senior Dancer, and cannot say whether the propensity to acquire was excited in the mind of the son, by the example of the parent, nor have we any memorial of the infancy and boyhood of this famous miser.

Upon the death of his father, Daniel Dancer came into possession of the paternal estate; the few hundreds which it annually produced was, by the strictest parsimony, and the most rigid saving, so increased as to produce, before he died, a revenue of three thousand pounds per annum. The sister of this singular character was as miserly as himself, and their habits and inclinations so harmonized, that after the death of their parents they always lived together, and strove during the whole of their lives to rival each other in their mode of scraping up and saving money.

The outward appearance of this amiable couple was such, that none could pass them without remark; and most could observe from their dress and manners indications of the presence of that sordid passion to which they devoted their entire lives, and to which they sacrificed every source of comfort and enjoyment. Daniel was his own tailor, and if he was not particularly happy in the style and cut of his garments, he at least displayed considerable ingenuity in the way of patching, repairing, and contriving; Jacob might have been proud, and Joseph vain of such a coat of many colours, as was the outer garment of Daniel Dancer; it was made of pieces of every hue, and fragments of every texture, collected from the streets, or raked out from the dust heaps. His lower garments were of the most unmentionable description, and would totally have disordered the nerves of any Scotchman; they were kept together by a strong hay-band girt round his waist, his stockings were so much darned, that it was difficult to discover any traces of the original, and in cold or wet weather, they were usually fortified and protected with ropes of twisted hay; by this novel and ingenious contrivance, he was enabled to save his boots; in fact, he was never known to spend a single shilling in shoe leather; now and then he would in his rambles pick up an odd shoe, which some poor cottager had thought too old for use; these were regarded by Dancer as great treasures, and he often spent his winter evenings in mending and patching them, for he was always his own cobbler. Linen was a luxury, says his biographer, to which, notwithstanding his avaricious disposition, he was not quite a stranger; for, at an early period of his saving career, he used to buy two shirts annually; but, for some years previous to his death, he never allowed himself more than one, for which he would give at some old clothes shop two shillings and sixpence, and was never once known to go to so handsome a price as three shillings; after it had got into his possession, it never underwent the necessary operation of either washing or mending; upon his back it was doomed to perpetual slavery, until it fell off in rags; hence, it will not be doubted, nor will it surprise the reader to be told, that notwithstanding Mr. Dancer's peculiarity of disposition induced him to shun the world, he never was without a numerous retinue about him; whose lively sport and attachment to his person, made his acquaintance as well as his neighbours, extremely cautious of approaching him.

Nor was Miss Dancer more scrupulous in her attire: she had but few feminine charms, and these few she made no attempts to adorn with the facination of dress. Her accoutrements were usually a mixture of male with female paraphernalia, tied round with a ravelling of hemp; for even in this part of her attire, she studied how to make one cord last longer by untwisting it to make it go further; and thus equipped, she would sally forth, armed with a broom-stick and pitch-fork, to check the progress of such daring marauders as had the audacity to intrude upon her brother's grounds—on which occasions, her neighbours observed she had more the appearance of a walking dunghill than of one of the fair sex.

The miserable hovel in which this eccentric, but harmonious pair, took up their abode, was perfectly in accordance with their appearance: no one could have passed it without thinking of poverty and squalidness: it was an eyesore to passers by, and a bugbear to the rising generation. The crazy window-sashes were paneless, and the loss of glass had been supplied with pieces of board, with paper and dirty rags. The tiles were loosened from the roof, and patches of unknown substances proclaimed the parsimony and ingenuity of the owner of the wretched habitation: the miser's house, in fact, was like the miser's coat, so patched and so slovenly repaired, that little of the original could be discovered; and its architecture appeared of the most novel and inventive kind.

Mr. Dancer's calculations for saving money were systematic and regular: nothing escaped his attention which had relation to this great object of his life—nothing ever too trivial for his care, and nothing too mean for his attention. So rigid was his parsimony, that he rarely washed his face and hands, because, as he said, soap was expensive, towels would wear out in time, and cost money to cleanse when dirty. It is said, however, that to avoid the inconvenience arising from a too great accumulation of filth, he would, once or twice a week, in the summer time, repair to a neighbouring pond, and there wash himself with sand, and afterwards lie on the bank to dry his skin by basking in the sunshine.

Dancer undoubtedly possessed an inventive genius, and his talents were great auxiliaries to his schemes of saving. If he felt the want of any article, he always endeavoured to make some other object answer the purpose, to obviate the necessity of expenditure. One day, by some strange chance, a neighbour entered the hovel of the miser: he found Mr. Dancer busily engaged pulling the nails out of the side of his bellows; and upon asking him the reason for so doing, he replied, that wanting some nails to fasten a piece of leather to a hole, which time had effected in the boarding of the house, he thought he could spare some out of that useful piece of household furniture, and, by that means, save buying; observing, at the same time, that undertakers, trunk-makers, and bellows-makers were the most extravagant and wasteful rascals in the world in their profusion of nails.

Daniel Dancer and his sister seem to have lived for no other purpose than to save money, nor to have had any other object than its accumulation. They had no thoughts, nor principles, nor rules of life, but such as were grounded upon the multiplication table. Every action of their life was to acquire, and their every thought was devoted to the study of the art of saving. They denied themselves any regular repast, but strove to vie with each other in their endeavours to lengthen the period between their meals. They never eat but when hunger compelled, and they never, in satisfying their hunger, indulged in the luxury of gratifying their appetite. Three pounds of coarse beef, and fourteen hard dumplings, formed their weekly provision for many years, without alteration or improvement. In hot weather, the meat appealed unpleasantly to the sense of smell, and advanced somewhat too far in the process of decomposition to have pleased a delicate appetite; but, as old Daniel used to observe on such occasions, that those who were devoted to saving, should feel satisfaction at these circumstances; for, if it did not improve the flavour of the meat, it rendered it more economical, because a less quantity proved sufficient; and, as none could be wasted, it lasted all the longer. Accident, or some unexpected fall of luck, would occasionally relieve this everlasting routine of hard dumplings. An uncommon instance (says his biographer) occurred one summer's morning, which, for many weeks, saved him the trouble of inquiring for fragments of meat at the butcher's stall, and which enabled him to gratify his darling avarice and insatiable propensity to save money. It happened one morning, as Mr. Dancer was taking his usual walk upon the common, to pick up bones, sticks, or any bit of rag or other matters that might go towards repairing his clothes or his house; that he found a sheep that had apparently died from natural disease, and most probably in a putrid state: this was a rare prize for Mr. Dancer; and incredible as it may appear, he took it up, and bore it home on his shoulders in triumph to his sister, who received it as the immediate gift of heaven to bless their poor souls with a change of food, and enable them to feast without expence, which was, to the appetite of a miser, the most savoury sauce that could accompany such a delicious morsel as carrion mutton. The sheep was immediately skinned and cut up, the fat was carefully laid aside, and, with the meat. Miss Dancer manufactured an immense number of pies; on these pies they feasted for many weeks—never departing from their accustomed frugality, and never indulging in any change of diet, until the whole stock was consumed. When a miser finds a treasure he is sure to lock it up; he is nervous whilst the eyes of strangers are upon it, and he never thinks it safe unless bars or bolts protect it. Dancer, therefore, soon locked up his pies in his strong chest, much to the annoyance of his fair sister; for the neighbours one morning observing that lady rather low spirited, kindly inquired into the cause, when, after some hesitation, she acknowledged that her brother Daniel had scolded her for feasting upon the mutton pies with too voracious an appetite, and accused her of extravagance, which she observed with tears, was an exceedingly hard case, as she loved to save as well as himself; but what vexed her more, he had locked them up in his strong trunk. It was seldom that such precaution was necessary, for she appears to have been as totally absorbed by the spirit of acquisitiveness as her brother; they were children of the same parents, and never were two beings in their devotion to mammon, and in their inordinate avarice, born with such an exact resemblance. Their tastes and their disposition, their opinions and principles were in perfect harmony. The miser is ever a stranger to piety, and religion is at variance with the professed object of his life. Whenever Mr.

Dancer happened to stray into a church, it was only to obtain a little rest, and he was sure to depart before any collection was made; as he thought the gift of a penny was like parting with the seed of a guinea. He might, indeed, be deemed a predestinarian from the following circumstance. But as Mr. Locke observes, "Let ever so much probability hang on one side, a covetous man's reasoning, and money on the other, it is easy to foresee which will outweigh." It was during the last illness which terminated his sister's life, that he was importuned to afford her some medical advice and assistance; to which he shrewdly replied, "It would cost him money, and besides," continued he, "why should I waste my money in wickedly and wantonly trying to oppose the will of God! If the girl has come to her latter end, nothing can save her, and all I may do will only tend to make me lose my money; and she may as well die now as at any other time. If I thought bleeding would recover her, I would open a vein myself; but I cannot think of paying for physic for dying people." The dread of incurring expence, and parting with his darling coin, was insurmountable. Mr. Dancer's reasoning on the conduct of Providence, ever tended towards his favourite penchant—"Save money."

Perhaps never having felt the inconvenience of ill health, or, from that callosity of heart ever attendant upon an avaricious mind; he at this period allowed his sister, in her last exigency, but the usual portion of coarse beef, with the cold hard dumpling, to which he added the miser's humanity—"If you don't like it, why go without." But Mr. Dancer's deficiency of care was very amply supplied by the generous Lady Tempest, who afforded every attention and kindness necessary to the case of Miss Dancer. The latter was possessed of more than two thousand pounds, which she intended to leave Lady Tempest, for her extraordinary care in her last illness; but she, unfortunately for Lady Tempest, expired before she could sign a will in her favour; and her property being thus left intestate, and at the disposition of the law, her two other brothers wished equally to divide it with Mr. Dancer; but to this proposal he would not agree, and obstinately refused to comply with any amicable arrangement; insomuch that, after a long while persevering, and obstinately refusing to come to any agreement of participation, a law suit followed, and Mr. Dancer recovered ten hundred and forty pounds of his sister's fortune, as the regular price of her board and lodging for thirty years, at thirty pounds per annum, and one hundred pounds for the last two years; for this charge he declared to be very reasonable, as during that time she had done nothing but eat and lie in bed. The remainder of her estate, after these extraordinary deductions, was equally divided between the two brothers and Mr. Dancer.

After his sister's death, a pair of sheets, as black as soot bags, were discovered upon the bed; but these he would never suffer to be removed; and when they were worn out, they were never replaced; so that, after that time, he entirely relinquished the luxury of using linen to sleep in. He would not allow any one to make his bed, although Lady Tempest often solicited him to permit it; and for many years his room was never swept. Towards the time of his death, it was observed to be filled with sticks, which he had stolen out of the different hedges. A considerable quantity of odd-shapen gravel stones were also found in a bag; but for what use these were intended is unknown. The report of his riches, and the idea of its concealment about the house, once brought a troop of housebreakers, who very easily entered, and without any search warrant rumaged every corner of the place; but although this domiciliary visit cost some of them their lives, they took away but little property. Old Dancer had been long on his guard, and his mode of hiding was so peculiar to himself, that the grand object of the thieves was never discoverable by them. Mr. Dancer concealed his treasure where no one would have ever thought of seeking for it. Bank notes were usually deposited with the spiders, and hid amongst the cobwebs in the cowhouse; and guineas in holes in the chimney, and about the fireplace, covered with soot and ashes. Soon after the robbery, when the thieves were apprehended, and to be tried, it being very necessary that Mr. Dancer should attend the trial, Lady Tempest requested that, in order to appear a little decent, he would change his shirt, and she would lend him a clean one. "No, no," he replied, "it is not necessary;" the shirt I have on is quite new, I bought it only three weeks ago, and then it was clean."

This extreme love of money overcame every other consideration; and to his attachment to gain may be accounted his strange behaviour as before related, to his sister at her latter end. But in one singular instance he seemed in some measure to forego his favourite idea of saving. He had a dog, of which he was extremely fond, and which he called by the familiar appellation of "Bob." His treatment of this animal offers an instance of that inconsistency in human actions, which philosophy seeks in vain to account for. "While his parsimony was so severe, that he denied himself a penny loaf a day, and existed entirely upon Lady Tempest's pot liquor, and the scraps from her kitchen; he allowed his dog a pint of milk daily, with other dainties, which he would have thought a sinful waste to have procured for himself. Upon a complaint being made to him that his favourite Bob had worried some of his neighbour's sheep, he took the dog to a farrier's shop, and had all his teeth filed down. For this barbarous action he never assigned any reason; possibly it might be to prevent the like again, as he might shrewdly guess that any further damage from his dog's mischievous manner, might bring expenses upon him. His sister being dead and finding himself lonesome, he hired a man for his companion, and in his choice he showed much discernment; for his man

Griffiths was a proper counterpart of himself. When they went out, they took different roads, though both followed the same occupation; only that the servant indulged more taste for strong beer; a liquor which Mr. Dancer carefully avoided, as costing money; but Griffiths would tipple a little, which was the cause of much altercation, when these saving souls met, after their day's labour. However, Griffiths generally came loaded with bones, some of which having upon them still some fragments of flesh, served to heighten their repast, and to quiet his master's anger. This fellow had, by as severe a parsimony as that exercised by Mr. Dancer, contrived to accumulate five hundred pounds out of wages, which had never exceeded ten pounds per annum. At the time he lived with Mr. Dancer, he was upwards of sixty, and hired himself to him for eighteen pence a week."

Lady Tempest was the only person who had any influence on this unfortunate miser. She employed every contrivance to make him partake of those conveniences and indulgences, which his fortune could supply, and his advanced years required; but all her entreaties were without effect, and were only answered with such interrogatories as, "Where was he to get the money?"—"How could he afford it? If it was not for some charitable assistance, how could he live?" One day however, this lady, after a great deal of persuasion, prevailed upon Dancer to purchase a hat, which he did of a Jew, for a shilling, having worn the one he then possessed upwards of fourteen years, but he still considered it too good to throw away. When Lady Tempest visited him the next time, she, to her great astonishment, perceived him still with his old hat on. On importuning him for the reason, he at last told her, that after much solicitation, he had prevailed on his old man Griffiths, to give him sixpence profit upon the hat he had purchased by her desire a few days before.

Mr. Dancer had arrived at his seventy-eighth year, before he felt any serious cause of complaint, to call in a doctor; his antipathy to the medical tribe has been already mentioned; therefore it was in vain to advise him to take any medicine, even when there was a necessity for it.

In 1794, during the illness which terminated the life of this miserable object of avarice, Lady Tempest accidentally called upon him, and found him lying in an old sack, which came up to his chin, and his head wrapped up in pieces of the same materials, as big as a bee hive. On her remonstrating against the impropriety of such a situation, he observed, that being a very poor man he could not afford better; and, having come into the world without a shirt, he was determined to go out in the same manner. As he brought nothing with him, he did not think he had any right to carry anything away; and the less he made use of he thought was the more acceptable to God; so that, in his last moments, he made his saving notions square with his most serious thoughts. Lady Tempest then requested him to have a pillow to raise his head, which he refused, but ordered his old servant Griffiths to bring him some litter out of the stable to raise his head, as the lady thought he would lie easier.

Though Mr. Dancer never indulged himself in the extravagant luxury of snuff-taking, yet he was careful always to solicit a pinch or two from those who did; but it was not to gratify his own nose, but rather to gratify, in a minor point of view, his love of hoarding; all that he collected by these friendly offerings, he carefully saved up and put into a box, which he carried about him for that purpose; and when full he would barter its contents at a neighbouring chandler's shop for a farthing candle, which he made last until he had replenished his box again.

His opinion of professors of physic was rather singular, and seemed to border upon predestination. To use his own language, the medical tinkers were all a set of rogues; that while they patched up one hole, always contrived to make two, for a better job; but he allowed that there was some utility in the art of surgery, in repairing accidental fractures; but he always qualified the admission with the reflection that its practitioners were a set of extortioners.

His prejudice against the whole tribe of lawyers was determined in the extreme, and his aversion to this class of men was so great, that he would even forego his own interest, to gratify his resentment; as the following anecdote will prove.

"Having, as was usually his half yearly custom, agreed with an old clothes woman for a shirt for half a crown, as he thought, the dealer called at his house, and left him one worth three shillings; but for which he refused to pay any more than his original agreement of two shillings and sixpence. Notwithstanding the party urged the goodness and the fineness of the article Mr. Dancer was impenetrable, and no more than the half crown would he pay; which the woman as peremptorily refusing, at last applied to the Court of Requests of the district, to which he was obliged to repair, although it cost him fivepence on the journey for bread and cheese, and the cost of hearing, &c.; in all upwards of four and sixpence." This had such an effect on Mr. Dancer's mind, that he ever afterwards held the lawyers in abhorrence; for to give or to pay, were not to be found in his vocabulary. Addition and multiplication were his favourite rules, and usury was the foundation of his good deeds.

"The most delightful task of Mr. Dancer's life was to count his gold, and to visit the holes where it lay deposited, and to see that all was safe. Upon one of these nocturnal visits he was not a little frightened: while counting the contents of one of his rich pots in the cow-house; a large tom cat, terrified at his untimely appearance in that place of concealment, and rushing through a hole in the boarding, left Mr. Dancer in such panic, that he thought Old Nick himself was watching his motions. To add to his terror, in returning back to the house he fell over something soft, which proved at last to be a poor jackass lying upon the ground, that had strayed in through one of the many apertures time had made in the enclosure of the estate."

Though Mr. Dancer, by his spirit of covetousness, debased himself in this sordid manner, yet he kept a horse, for which he showed a great partiality; but he never allowed it more than two shoes at a time, deeming it an unnecessary expense to shoe the hind feet of the animal; and he used to say it was more pleasant for a horse to feel the naked grass than to be confined in unnatural shoes.

Mr. Dancer was, perhaps, the most perfect picture of human penury that ever existed, and the most singular character that ever lived; his habits were those of an hermit, and his extreme avarice rendered him as abstemious as any ascetic of the desert. In this state lived, and in this situation died, Daniel Dancer Esq., a memorable proof to the world, that the advantages of fortune, unless properly directed, will not make their possessor happy. Lady Tempest, who came into possession of a great portion of the miser's property, enjoyed it but for a short time; for whilst attending to the comforts of Dancer during his last illness she caught a cold which terminated fatally, a few months after her accession to the immense fortune left by the old miser.

The house, or rather the heap of ruins, in which Mr. Dancer lived, and which at his death devolved to the right of Captain Holmes, was a most miserable decayed building, for it had not been repaired for more than half a century. But though poor in external structure, the ruinous fabric was very rich in the interior. It took many weeks to explore its whole contents; and Captain Holmes found it a very agreeable task to dive into the miser's secret hoards. One of Mr. Dancer's richest escritoires was found to be a dung heap in the cowhouse; a sum but little short of two thousand five hundred pounds was contained in this rich piece of manure; and in an old jacket carefully tied, and strongly nailed down to the manger, in bank notes and gold, were found five hundred pounds more. Several bowls were discovered filled with guineas and half-guineas; and at different times, on searching the corners of the house, they found various parcels of bank notes. Some were crammed into the crevices in the wall; bundles were hid under the cushions and covers of the chairs; some were reposing snugly at the back of the drawers; and notes amounting to six hundred pounds were found neatly doubled up, in the inside of an old tea-pot, over which the miser had placed a bit of paper, whimsically inscribed, "not to be too hastily looked over." In the stable the Captain found jugs full of old dollars and shillings. It was observable that Mr. Dancer used to visit this place in the dead of the night; but for what purpose even old Griffiths himself could not guess; but it is supposed it was to rob one jug, to add to a bowl he had buried, and which was nearly full when taken up from under one of the hearth tiles.

The chimney was not left unsearched, and paid very well for the trouble; for in nineteen different holes, all filled with soot, were found various sums of money, amounting together to more than two hundred pounds.

CHAPTER IX

LIFE OF JOHN ELWES.

The character of John Elwes—Sir Harvey Elwes—His singular habits—His dress—Three Knights quarrel about a farthing—Mrs. Meggot, the mother of John Elwes, starves herself to death, although possessed of a fortune of One Hundred Thousand Pounds—The love of Play in John Elwes—His inconsistency of character—Generosity in a Miser—How to save a toll—His conscientious disposition—The passion of avarice—His old age—The Miser rescued when at the point of death—His last days—His death, &c.

LIFE OF JOHN ELWES.

The life of John Elwes has been so minutely recorded in an amusing narrative, by Captain Topham, and extracts from that work have been so frequently reprinted, that we were prone to exclude his name from our Lives and Anecdotes of Misers. It was some years ago that we read the book, and we found on glancing over it again the other day, that there were many anecdotes in his Memoirs, which so illustrate the passion of avarice, as to render the life of John Elwes especially deserving a notice from our hands. Mr. Elwes was a miser in the fullest acceptation of the term, and to obtain gold there was no sacrifice that he thought too great; yet he possessed qualities and traits of amiability, that won for him, in spite of his ruling vice, the respect and friendship of many worthy men.

Before we relate some singular anecdotes of this miser for the amusement of our readers, it will be as well to notice the memorable eccentricities of his uncle, Sir Harvey Elwes. On succeeding to the family estate, the knight became nominally possessed of some thousands a year, but really only of an income of one hundred pounds per annum. He said on his arrival at Stoke in Suffolk, the family seat, that never would he leave it until he had entirely cleared the paternal estate. For more than sixty years he lived there, almost alone; grasping, screwing, and scraping, to accumulate wealth. He received no visitors; he enjoyed no luxuries; and worst of all deprivations, he read no books! He was never seen with a volume in his hand; his scholarship was wholly devoted to the decyphering of old deeds, and in composing usurious bonds. In his housekeeping, like all misers, he was wretchedly penurious, and in his dress he would have suited admirably for one of Garrick's most ludicrous characters. He wore a black velvet cap, which being vastly too large, constantly fell over his eyes; an old time-worn suit of dress clothes, with worsted stockings drawn over the knees; these garments cost him nothing, for he took them from an old chest, where they had lain ever since the gay days of his father, Sir Jarvas Elwes. When the weather was cold, Sir Harvey would walk briskly, backwards and forwards in his old hall, to save the expense of firing; and if a farmer came on business, he would strike a light in a tinder-box, which he always kept by him, and putting one solitary stick in the huge old-fashioned grate, would not add another till the first had been nearly consumed.

Notwithstanding his dislike to society, Sir Harvey would occasionally venture a portion of his wealth at the gaming table; in fact, with the most miserly parsimony, the knight combined the restless disposition of the gambler. Sir Cordwell Firebras, and Sir John Barnardiston, were neighbours of Sir Harvey's, and from a similarity of tastes they became close companions; they used to meet at the little village of Stoke, and play a few rubbers of whist. When they parted, the reckoning was always divided between them with the most scrupulous exactitude, and the fractions of a penny were objects of serious consideration. One day, when they were engaged in settling some such difficult point, a wag called out to a friend that was passing, "Step up stairs, and assist the poor! Here are three baronets, each worth a million of money, quarrelling about a farthing."

Sir Harvey usually had large sums of money in the house, amounting to three or four thousand pounds at a time. A set of desperate burglars, dreaded and known throughout the country as the Thackstead gang, hearing of this circumstance, formed a plan to rob him. The old house was easily invaded, and the two servants were gagged and threatened if they attempted resistance. They presented their pistols to Sir Harvey, and demanded his money; he gave them the key of a drawer, in which they found fifty guineas. They were dissatisfied, and threatened instantly to take his life if he did not deliver up his hoards. After many protestations of poverty, he at last submitted to the urgent necessity of the case, and pointed out the hiding-place of his treasure, in which were found twenty-seven hundred guineas. On quitting, they told him that they should leave a man behind, who would murder him if he called for assistance. Sir Harvey, with admirable simplicity quietly took out his watch and said, "Gentlemen, I do not want to take any of you, therefore I will give you twenty minutes to escape."

When this gang of thieves some years afterwards were captured, Sir Harvey revised to appear against them; and when urged to go to Chelmsford to identify them, he would reply, "No, no! I have lost my money, and now you want me to lose my time also."

Many are the anecdotes preserved of this singular man, but we are compelled to leave them, to record those related of his nephew and successor.

The sister of Sir Harvey Elwes married a Mr. Meggot, a wealthy brewer of Southwark, who died a few years after his marriage, leaving a son, and one hundred thousand pounds to his widow. Mrs. Meggot, like her brother, was of a most miserly disposition; and although possessed of so ample a fortune, is said to have actually starved herself to death! Sir Harvey left to her son, John Meggot, the whole of his vast possessions, which were then estimated at two hundred and fifty thousand pounds; and he directed that his nephew was thereupon to assume the name and arms of the Elwes'. Mr. Elwes was about forty years of age at his uncle's death; and previous to this period he had entered into many of the gaities of life, and became known to the fashionable and sporting circles in London. He had always, however, paid great deference to his uncle's foibles, and was always anxious to ingratiate himself in his favour, by assuming an aspect of the most rigid parsimony. On paying Sir Harvey a visit, he used to dress as a perfect miser; a tattered waistcoat, a worn-out coat, stockings darned with the most persevering industry, fastened with a pair of small iron buckles; when thus arrayed, the uncle used to contemplate his future heir with unfeigned delight, and was enraptured to find in him so striking a resemblance of himself.

Mr. Elwes had always a turn for play; in his time the gaming-table was a fashionable resort, and he was one of the most celebrated players of his day; few men had played deeper than himself. He once played two days and two nights without intermission; the room being a small one, and of course, never using the same pack a second time, they were nearly up to their knees in cards. He lost many thousands at that sitting; the Duke of Northumberland was of the party, who was never known to quit a table while there was any hopes of winning. We thus observe in the life of John Elwes, a remarkable instance of the analogy which appears to exist between the gambler and the miser. The love of play and the love of saving are both the promptings of avarice, and are both indications of an undue excitement of the acquisitive propensity.

> "The ruling passion, be it what it will,
> The ruling passion conquers Reason still."

"It is curious," says Captain Topham, "to remark, how he contrived to mingle small attempts at saving, with objects of the most unbounded dissipation. After sitting up whole nights, staking thousands with the most fashionable and profligate men of his day, amid splendid rooms, gilt sofas, wax lights, and waiters, he would walk out about four in the morning, not towards home, but into Smithfield, to meet his own cattle, which were coming to market from Thaydon Hall, a farm of his in Essex. There would the man, forgetful of the scenes he had just left, stand in the cold or rain, haggling with a carcase butcher for a shilling. Sometimes when the cattle did not arrive at the hour appointed he would walk on to meet them; and has more than once gone on foot the whole way to his farm, which was seventeen miles from London, after sitting up the whole of the night. Yet this remarkable man, who

In the way of a bargain.
He'd cavil on the ninth part of a hair.

Shakespeare.

could be generous at times; several instances of his liberality are recorded, which are curious to observe in one so habitually parsimonious. On one of his excursions to Newmarket, he found that Lord Abingdon had made a match for seven thousand pounds, which, it was supposed he would be obliged to forfeit, from inability to produce the sum, though the odds were greatly in his favour. Unsolicited, Mr. Elwes offered him the money, which was accepted, and his lordship won the engagement. On another occasion he advanced a large sum of money to a gentleman of the name of Tempest, to purchase a commission in the guards; he lent the money without security and never asked him for its repayment, yet he had only seen him once or twice."

John Elwes was a singular illustration of the inconsistency of the human mind. "One day a Mr. Spurling accompanied him to Newmarket, to be present at the spring races. They were out from six in the morning, and it was eight o'clock in the evening before they set out on their way home. Elwes, as usual, during the day eat nothing. When they began their journey home the evening was dark and very cold, and Mr. Spurting rode on somewhat quicker; and on going through the turnpike, by the "devil's ditch," he heard Mr. Elwes calling to him with great eagerness. On returning before he had paid the toll, Mr. Elwes said—"Here! here! follow me; this is the best road! "In an instant he saw Mr. Elwes, as well as the night would permit, climbing his horse up the precipice of the ditch. "Sir," said Mr. Spurling, "I can never get up there." " No danger at all!" replied old Elwes, "but if your horse be not safe, lead him!" At length, with great difficulty, they mounted the ditch, and then, with not less toil, got down on the other side. When they were safely landed on the plain, Mr. Spurling thanked Heaven for their escape. "Aye," said the miser, "you mean from the turnpike. Very right; never pay a toll if you can avoid it." It is a curious fact, that at the very time when he thus ventured his life to save a paltry toll, he was actually engaged in a speculation connected with some American iron works, risking the enormous sum of twenty-five thousand pounds; and upon which he had entered without apparently much consideration, for he knew nothing as to the produce, prospects, or situation of these mines, but what he had gleaned from hearsay. With all his vices John Elwes, it must be owned, was remarkably conscientious; if by any chance he became indebted, he was never easy till he had paid; and he was never known if he promised payment, to fail in fulfilling his engagement.

Mr. Elwes had resided thirteen years in Suffolk, when he was proposed as a representative in Parliament. He used to boast that all the expense incurred in his election was eighteenpence, which he paid for dining at an ordinary at Reading. Mr. Elwes was about sixty when he thus entered into public life; he sat in Parliament as the member for Berkshire, for more than twelve years, but during the whole of that time he never delivered a speech. Although remarkably attentive to his parliamentary duties, he was never known to indulge, even when the weather was the most uncomfortable, in the luxury of a cab; and after staying out the debate, he would walk home, through cold and wet, to save coach hire. Some of the members who happened to be going the same way, would propose a coach between them, but Elwes always replied that he liked nothing so much as walking. At length he retired to his seat at Stoke; and on arriving there he remarked, "That he had lost a great deal of money very foolishly, but that a man grew wiser in time."

And now in his declining years he became totally involved by his mammon worship. His appetite for other pleasures had diminished. The gaming-table had failed to excite his cupidity; the race course had lost its attractions, and society no longer possessed a charm; but whilst these sources of former joy were no longer sought; whilst these desires had become extinguished by years, or chilled as the winter of life approached, his lust and insatiable avarice for gold remained vigorous in his old age, and green and flourishing amidst the wintry barrenness which had overtaken the other vices and passions of his mind. No ray of his better nature appeared—the energies and thoughts of his old age were devoted to the acquisition of wealth; and Mr. Elwes, now worth nearly a million of money, became the saver of pence. He used to wander about the fields and roads to pick up sticks, bones or pieces of rag; during the harvest month he would condescend to mingle with the village gleaners, and carry home the result of his labours to store away for the use of his own household. He would breakfast on a piece of stale pancake, or crust of dry bread; and on more than one occasion almost starved himself by his own extreme habits of penury.

Mr. Elwes, when in London, usually occupied any one of his own houses that happened to be unlet. Knowing that Elwes was in town, a Colonel Tims was very anxious to see him, but could not obtain his address; at last he accidentally heard that he was seen to go into an uninhabited house in Great Marlborough Street, and he ascertained from a pot-boy that an old woman generally opened the stable-door to admit Mr. Elwes. He repaired thither, and knocked loudly at the door, but could gain no admittance; he deter- mined to have the stable-door opened; a blacksmith was sent for, and they entered the house together; ascending the stairs, they heard the moans of some one seemingly indisposed, and went into the chamber, and there, upon a squalid mattress lay the apparently lifeless body of old Elwes. There was nothing near him but a part of a stale roll and a jug of cold water. An apothecary was called in, and after a time the miser recovered enough to say, that he believed he had been ill for two or three days, and that there was an old woman in the house, but for some reason or other she had not been near him; that she had been ill herself, but had got well, and he supposed she had gone away. On entering the garret the old woman was found lifeless on a mat upon the floor, and to all appearances had been dead about two days: yet at the time of this occurrence Mr. Elwes was one of the richest men of his day, and possessed so many houses in London, that he became from calculation his own insurer.

As his end approached he had many warnings of coming dissolution; his nights were broken and restless, and he frequently arose to satisfy himself that his money was safe, and he was sometimes heard as if struggling with some one in his chamber, and crying out, "I will keep my money; no one shall rob me of my property." On any one going into his room he started alarmed, and as if waking from a troubled dream, would appear surprised, and quietly retire again to his bed seeming totally unconscious of what had happened. In the autumn of 1789 his mind began to waver; his memory became impaired, and his reason rapidly declined. A propensity which had long been over active and diseased, now became fearfully violent by the excitement of insanity. For many weeks before his death he used to go to bed in his clothes as perfectly dressed as in the day-time. One morning he was found in his bed fast asleep with his shoes on, a stick in his hand, and an old hat on his head. The anxieties and feverish excitement which his passion for gold produced, tended to shorten his life. When Dr. Wells, his last physician, was called in, and found him extended on his miserable pallet, denying himself every comfort, and with his mind totally absorbed with his gold, he turned to one of the sons of Mr. Elwes, and said, "Sir, your father might have lived these twenty years, but his temper has made it impossible to hope for anything; the body is yet strong, but the mind is gone entirely." He died quietly on the 18th of November, 1789, but without any indication of repentance, without any signs of a diminution of his avarice, or without any thoughts of the future. In his last words addressed to his son he expressed a hope "that he had left him what he wished." He bequeathed the whole of his vast fortune, amounting in addition to his estate, to the sum of five hundred thousand pounds, to his two natural sons, George and John Elwes.

Thus died John Elwes, the representative of a family of misers. He began, as we have seen, his career as a gambler, in which he displayed his innate avarice, modified by his contact with the vices of fashionable life; for amidst the most boundless profligacy at the gaming-table, we have seen that acquisitiveness was ever active, and his mind was always on the watch to save.

Search the Ruling Passion. There alone,
The wild are constant, and the cunning known;

The fool consistent and the false sincere;
Priests, princes, women, no dissemblers here.

POPE.

CHAPTER X

NOTICES OF FEMALE MISERS.

Mary Luhorne, the Female Miser of Deptford; her Miserable Habits of Penury; her Love of Hoarding; her enormous Wealth—Elizabeth Wilcocks and her Secret Hoards—The Misses Vooght, Three Female Misers of Amsterdam; a singular instance of Avarice as a Family failing—Joanna Horrel the Applewoman of Exeter; her sumptuous fortune, &c.

NOTICES OF FEMALE MISERS.

It has been remarked, that when women become vicious they know no medium; they are good or they are very bad; and when once fascinated with vice, they are more difficult to reclaim than men. Certainly, in the cases which we subjoin of female misers, the passion of avarice appears in fearful strength, rendering the heart of its votaries callous to the call of duty, and insensible to the dictates of conscience.

In the month of August of the year 1766 there died at Deptford a wretched old woman, in her ninety-sixth year; she was the widow of Captain Luhorne, of the East India service. She survived her husband forty years, and during the whole of that period she lived in a most miserly and penurious manner. She not only denied herself the comforts, but even the most common necessaries and decencies of life. Her clothes were so tattered that she was almost in a state of nudity, and the rags which she hung upon her shoulders were so filthy, and so animated with vermin, that passengers took the precaution to keep at a distance from her in the streets. She was never known to have lit a fire in her room, and never indulged in the luxury of a candle; she wore no under garments, and had no sheet to cover her at night; she eschewed all rules of cleanliness, and appeared never so happy as when surrounded with filth and loathsomeness. She would frequently wander along the roads to beg of passers by, and always professed the utmost poverty. The demon of avarice was so strong within this covetous soul, that she was more than once detected in pilfering some trifling articles from her neighbours. One Tuesday the old woman was missed; she had not been observed to leave her room, and she had not been seen in her accustomed walks: Wednesday past, and the neighbours began to suspect that the old miser must be ill; they knocked at her door, but no voice replied; they waited for the morrow; and when the day had far advanced, and she did not appear, they got in at the window. They found her in bed alive, but speechless: with attention she revived a little, but on Saturday the old woman died. Her relatives were sent for, who on opening her drawers and chests found securities and gold to the amount of forty thousand pounds, besides clothes of the most sumptuous make and texture, plate, china, jewels and linen. For years had she been surrounded with this wealth and possessed these luxuries, which if rightly used would have served to comfort her old age, and have been the means of relieving the miseries and wants of others; the remembrance would in return have proved a great solace to the bed of sickness and death. Yet although her drawers were thus crammed with costly apparel, which was slowly mouldering and rotting before the effects of time; that wretched object of penury chose rather to wear rags so filthy that it became the imperative duty of her relatives to bum them immediately after her death.

In a life so wretched—so devoid of purpose, so laborious, without an object, so self-denying and so debased—we have a striking example of the littleness of human wishes, and the ignobility of the human mind, when unguided by reason, and when swayed by the despotism of the passions. Her life is, indeed, a problem the philosopher will find some difficulty to solve. With forty thousand pounds, no fraction of which she would venture to enjoy—with none for whom affection would prompt her to save—here was a wretched being whose lust for gold, and whose propensity to hoard, was so overwhelming, that she would beg of strangers in the streets—pilfer whatever she could lay her hands upon; and although surrounded with an abundance, deprived herself of every enjoyment—of every hope and consolation—that she might gratify this most senseless propensity of her nature. When we think of the worthlessness of her life—of her avarice, as manifested in all its strength at the age of ninety-five, and of her lonely and comfortless death-bed—we are prompted to exclaim, with the psalmist, Vanitas vanitatum omnia vanitas!

In the year 1768, there died at Nether-Shuckburgh, in Warwickshire, an old maid, named Elizabeth Wilcocks, whose life presents a similar illustration of that love of hoarding, and that passion to acquire, which we have seen exemplified so fearfully in the case of Mary Luhorne. For many years before her death, she eat nothing but horse-beans or a few curlings: she had hardly any clothes, and had nothing but a bundle of straw and an old blanket to lie upon; yet, at her death, twelve pairs of sheets, and a large quantity of other linen, was found in her drawers. She hid her wealth in the most unaccountable places. In a pickle-pot, stowed away in the clock-case, was discovered eighty pounds in gold and five pounds in silver. In a hole under the stairs a canister full of gold: in an old rat-trap a large quantity of gold and silver, and in several other places similar hoards were discovered by her executors. In addition to all this wealth, this miserable old miser was possessed of an estate in houses and land producing a handsome revenue. She left the whole of her property to a very distant relative.

In an old newspaper, called the "General Evening Post," of the date December 21, 1779, there is an announcement of the death of Miss Maria Vooght, the female miser, of Amsterdam. She was the last of three singular and parsimonious sisters.

Lest they should not be enabled to gratify their propensity to accumulate and save, they resolutely declined all offers of matrimony. They lived huddled together in one room—gloried, like true misers, in filth, and lumber, and vermin. They eat the coarsest food, and of that but sparingly, and they were never known to have bestowed a fraction in charity. There never, perhaps, were seen such miserable, dirty, and untidy old maids. In all three, the passion of avarice was equally strong: it appeared in them a family vice: they were not induced to become so parsimonious from the fear of any future want, for they had each a fortune which would have secured all those comforts and enjoyments it is in the power of gold to provide. Maria Vooght, the last of these eccentric characters, left at her death, a fortune of five millions of guilders, equal to five hundred thousand pounds. She died intestate, and the money went to strangers.

About forty years ago, the overseers of Horncastle summoned a poor man, named Daniel Collwood, for refusing to support his wife. He was asked why he had not done so, and he stated, in reply, that his wife took all the money she could obtain from him; but instead of applying it to domestic purposes, hoarded it away, but in what place he was unable to discover. The overseers ordered a search to be made. On entering the house, the woman, as usual, pleaded the utmost poverty, affirming that she was almost starving with hunger, and that she had not a single farthing in the house. They, much to her consternation, commenced a search, and soon found hid in various parts about one hundred and thirty-four pounds in specie, carefully wrapped up in small bits of paper and folded round with old rags! Yet, whilst this miserable being had been accumulating this sum, she had destroyed the domestic peace of her husband by spreading about a report that he refused to allow her the necessary means of subsistence.

Many years ago, there used to sit in the streets of Exeter an old woman selling lemons and apples. In the very hottest day she did not flinch before the sun; and in the very bitterest of December nights she was sure to be found at her accustomed place. Now and then she did business in her little way, and took a few coppers from the urchins in the streets. Her appearance bespoke the utmost poverty, and her rigid habits of parsimony were regarded by the charitable as the shifts of indigence. She had been an old inhabitant of the city, but all her relatives were poor, and one of them had long been an inmate of the workhouse. There were but few who, knowing these circumstances, did not pity poor old Joanna Horrel, the apple-woman, of Exeter; and loose halfpence were often quietly dropped into her fruit-basket. These tributes of compassion were always carefully hoarded up, and however much she obtained by such means, she never altered her appearance, never lived more generously, never indulged herself in luxuries or comforts at home, and never once thought of her poor relative in the poor-house. In the year 1789, Joanna had grown old, and her span of life was at an end. Her relatives came to fulfil the last duties for the dead, and on searching her room, hid here and there in cracks and corners, behind bricks and under the flooring, they discovered a fortune of near ten thousand pounds.

CHAPTER XI

THE INSANITY OF AVARICE.

Avarice in the Insane—Curious Anecdotes of Lunatics—The Miser of St. Petersburg—His singular Life, and enormous Wealth—His Loan to Catharine, Empress of Russia—The Miser's Watchdog—Its death—The Miser becomes his own Housedog to save the cost of another—Col. Dogherty of the Royal Marines—His singular character—Michael Dudley, the Irish Miser, and his one hundred pound note—The Miser of Bloomsbury—Sheldon, the Miser of Kentish Town—Indications of Insanity—The effects of Avarice on the Mind—Avarice a prolific cause of Insanity, &c.

THE INSANITY OF AVARICE.

Like all other faculties and propensities of the human mind, the mania to acquire sometimes becomes a mental disease, and outsteps the control of the better feelings. The asylums for the insane contain numerous and remarkable instances of the morbid workings of this ignoble love of gold. Wretches of the most abject misery—imbecile and insane—will sometimes display the utmost craft and circumspection in the gratification of this ruling passion of their minds. As a monomania, it is too lamentably common; for we must regard the man, who, whilst in possession of an ample fortune, still strives by the most sordid parsimony, and the most disreputable cunning, to increase his hoards, as one whose mind is impaired, or whose passion for gold has produced a mental aberration. The proprietor of a private lunatic asylum once related to us some singular anecdotes of this passion, as manifested by his unfortunate patients. One of them had been a noted miser years before he became an inmate of the asylum, and a sudden and unforeseen loss which he had sustained, was supposed to have been the cause of his insanity. His whole soul had been centred in his gold, and deprived of his treasure, his mind became a total wreck; in his lucid intervals he would grow desponding, and abandon himself to the most lamentable despair; he would pine and fret; sob like a child deprived of its bauble, and then, in the paroxysm of his grief, rave into frantic madness; clutch hold of his keepers and denounce them as robbers, and seeking some worthless object that happened to be at hand, he would guard it with the most tenacious ferocity, declaring that it was his bag of gold, and that he would rather part with life, than part with that. Another poor wretch used to wander about the garden of the asylum in search of pebbles, which happened by their rotundity to call up to his mind the recollection of coin; these he would seek for with persevering industry, and, when discovered, he would secret them about his clothes with the greatest caution, and after a time bury them in a particular spot in the garden, and lie always manifested the most intense anxiety if any of the other patients happened to wander near the place of his secret hoards. He was generally harmless in his manner, but he was always excited into passion, if by any chance his pursuits were interfered with, or his fictitious coin disturbed by his unfortunate companions.

Many years ago, there lived in a large, cheerless and dilapidated, old house in St. Petersburg, a wretched miser. He confined himself to one room, and left the rest of the rambling edifice to moulder into ruin; he cared for no comfort, and deprived himself even of those things which the poorest regard as the necessaries of life; he seldom lit a fire to repel the dampness, which, hung on the walls of his solitary chamber, and a few worthless objects of furniture was all that the room contained. Yet to this singular being the Empress Catherine the Second owed a million of rubles. His cellar, it was said, contained casks full of gold, and packages of silver were stowed away in the dismal corners of his ruinous mansion. He was one of the richest men in Russia. He relied, for the safety of his hoards, upon the exertions of a huge mastiff, which he had trained to bark and howl throughout the night, to strike terror into the hearts of thieves. The miser outlived the dog; but he disliked to part with any portion of his treasure in the purchase of another cur, and he resolved to save his money by officiating as his own watch dog. Every morning, and every evening, would that insane old man wander about his dismal habitation, barking and howling in imitation of his recent sentinel.

Perhaps a more decided manifestation of the insanity of avarice was exemplified in the life of lieutenant-Colonel O'Dogherty, of the Royal Marines. He died in February, 1819, near Landrake. For more than twenty years he was in the habit of visiting Plymouth Market, and he always made his appearance, mounted on an old hack as lean as Rosinante. The singularity of his dress, and the eccentricity of his manners, soon obtained for him the reputation of a miser. He generally wore a nightcap, tied round his head, which had evidently been for years a stranger to the wash-tub; an old hat, quite bare of nap, and brimless; a rough waistcoat, the original texture of which it would have puzzled the most sagacious to have discovered—so numerous were its patches and so various its hues; a greasy leather pair of breeches; an old coat, which no Jew would have rescued from the kennel, and a pair of shattered shoes bound round with huge haybands, formed the usual habiliments of this singular character. On his last visit to Plymouth, a week or two before his death, thus arrayed, he seated himself on the steps of the Plymouth Telegraph Office to eat an apple, which probably, was designed to satisfy his hunger during the greatest portion of the day. Yet, whilst practising this wretched penury, he possessed freehold property of considerable value, amply sufficient to have maintained him in comfort, and in a dignity befitting the squire of his village. He chose, however, to forsake the family mansion, and took up his abode in a small cottage in its immediate vicinity. A most wretched hovel it was, without a pane of glass in the windows, but with innumerable inconvenient apertures in the roof. He always kept the door closely barred and blocked up, and he used to get in and out of his house through the bedroom window, with the aid of a ladder; this he would at night draw up after him, and seek his repose on a bundle of dirty straw, huddled into one corner of his room.

We may observe too, indications of an unsound mind in the senseless manner in which some misers have been known to gratify their love of hoarding; in the case of John Little, and several others, mentioned in our former chapters, we have seen the miser gratifying his propensity to hoard, when, by so doing, he necessarily entailed a pecuniary loss. We have a curious illustration of this, in the case of Michael Dudley, an Irishman, who was robbed in the year 1831. It seems, from the report of the trial of the thieves, which appeared in the papers of the time, that he had been robbed of an old pocket book, containing notes to the value of one hundred and sixty pounds, among which there was one note for a hundred pounds, that he had carried about with him for seventeen years. He came possessed of it by a legacy, and nothing could induce him to part with it for a note of more modem currency, or to place it out at interest. This old man had been for many years a boot cleaner at the Castle Tavern, in Exeter-street, Dublin, and he was constantly seen wandering about the streets, dressed in a miserable tattered suit of clothes, which, many years ago, had been given to him out of charity. He seldom purchased a meal, but strove to satisfy the cravings of nature by pickings from the refuse of the market stalls, or by begging a few scraps of the inhabitants. He lived in a garret, in a dismantled, uninhabited old tenement, in Sycamore-lane, a perfect slave to self-sacrifice and self-denial.

A rich capitalist, named M. Thibaudard, died a few years ago, at Paris, leaving an immense sum of money; some of which was found hoarded away in the most unaccountable places rendering it doubtful whether the whole of his properly was ever discovered. He had a residence in the country, but he hired a room in Paris, which he used frequently to visit. He died, and left his wife residuary legatee. A few weeks after his death, she went to Paris, to the room before alluded to. The weather was cold, and she had a fire lit, but as the smoke poured from the fireplace, and filled the room, she sent for a sweep, who examined the chimney, when, at a considerable height, he found a leather valise, containing twenty thousand francs, gold coins, and a large quantity of precious stones. It is evident, that the man who would thus place his property in jeopardy, must, as it were, have been on the verge of insanity.

Some two or three years ago, a miserable old man died in the metropolis, leaving behind him an ample fortune. For many years he had been in the habit of rising at an early hour in the morning, and sallying out to search the streets for bits of bone or rags; he always bent his steps towards Covent Garden market, and from the refuse of the stalls, he would carry home a quantity of fragments of potatoes, carrots, and other vegetables, which, in the course of the day, he would stew down, and form into a dainty dish. He always walked along the streets with his eyes upon the ground; no pin escaped his vigilant eye; no piece of paper was passed without being examined; no fragment of twine, no stray remnant of cloth or rag, was allowed to repose in the kennel; sometimes he was rewarded by the discovery of some article of greater value, and he used to boast that he had found several pieces of jewellery in the vicinity of the theatres. He lived in a room, in a house in Gilbert-street, Bloomsbury; the house was his own, and he had several others in the same street, and considerable sums of money in the funds, or, stowed away in his own house. He seldom purchased provisions, but managed to eke out a subsistence from his gatherings in the streets; sometimes he bought a stale loaf, or a small quantity of butter, at a chandler's shop in the neighbourhood, and his constant remark was, "never mind how rank it is, so as it is cheap." In this case, avarice became so strong, as to overwhelm the mind, and the old man died at an advanced age, imbecile and insane.

A few weeks ago, an old miser, of the name of Sheldon, died at Blandford-place, Kentish Town. He has left it is supposed, about twenty thousand pounds; yet this miserable slave to mammon would wander about the adjacent streets, to pick up any rubbish that could be turned into money, or any fragments that would help to form a meal; he had often been seen pick up bits of bread or potatoe from the mud in the streets, and carry them home, when he would wash them, and afterwards eat them with a relish; he was insensible to all notions of refinement or decency, and for twenty years he never allowed his room to be swept. He seldom wore a hat, and in the coldest weather he refused to allow himself a coat. He never washed his face but once a month, and then only when urged to do so by constant importunities. Often have we seen him perambulating the roads about Kentish Town, with a crowd of boys behind him, hooting and exasperating the old miser into a passion, but even in the midst of his perplexity, and when his rage was at its height, if a bone or a piece of rag happened to meet his eye, he would forget his passion and his tormentors in his eagerness to obtain it. Habits of parsimony seem conducive to longevity, for he died at the advanced age of eighty-five. He had no relations that have yet been discovered, and his ample fortune is destined to be locked up in Chancery, or to go to strangers whom he had never seen.

Such instances are evident indications of insanity; we behold in them the moral powers of the mind; all those social faculties which elevate man so immeasurably above the brute, ruled despotically by an inordinate passion to acquire. There are few passions, indeed, the abuse of which so endanger the equilibrium of the human mind, as that of avarice, and, in a great commercial country like our own, the prevalence of this feeling leads to incalculable misery, both individually and nationally. The endless solicitude—the feverish excitement—the harassing competition—the speculating nature of commercial enterprise, and the wear and tear incidental to these things, make the young man forget the dreams of youth, and the old man the remembrance of the tomb. The soul becomes enthralled by schemes of gain; social joys and domestic duties are forgotten; like an ill-regulated clock, the countenance bears false evidence of years; premature wrinkles, lines of anxious thought, point to a premature old age, and to an early grave. We are not indifferent to the blessing of commerce; we are not insensible of the necessity for exertion which exists, and we have no word of blame for those struggling to obtain an honourable livelihood. But, without arrogating to ourselves the office of a monitor, we would gently remind him, who has allowed avarice to usurp the place of legitimate enterprise, of the perils which he is weaving around him. Let him think for a moment, of the fiery ordeal through which he must pass to accomplish his schemes of avarice. Let him dwell for a moment upon the sacrifice of peace of mind, on the loss of health, on the nights of unquiet sleep, on the torturing disappointments, on the anxious fears, and the almost certain fate of an early death which the lust for gold entails. Let him then cast up the profits of this misery and toil; draw up within his mind a balance sheet, debit to himself on the one side, the probable consequences which we have enumerated, and credit to himself on the other, the bags of gold which peradventure he may accumulate; the interest they may produce in the few short years which he may have to live; the sum total of the fortune which he will be able to leave for his heir to spend. Weigh both sides, examine every item, and strike a balance. Choose between bags of unused gold, an unquiet life, an early grave; or a healthy life, a peaceful old age, and a happy death-bed.

It may, perhaps, influence the decision of those who will condescend to draw up, within their minds, such a balance sheet, to know that no propensity or faculty is so liable to disease as that of acquisitiveness; that the inordinate pursuit of wealth produces more mental dissolution, more mental calamities, and more insanity, than does the abuse of any other passion of the human mind. In a table, compiled by M. Esquirol, it appeared that one hundred and sixty-four cases of insanity bore the following proportions: fifty of them were merchants, thirty-three were military men, twenty-five were students, twenty-one administrateurs, ten were advocates, eight artists, four chemists, four were doctors, four were farmers, three were sailors, and two were engineers. This preponderance of merchants, or of those manifesting most actively the love of gain, and the most eager in the pursuit of wealth, was fully borne out by an examination of the patients in other lunatic asylums. Merchants formed by far the largest proportion of the insane in all the establishments. M. Fodere attributes this circumstance to the "chances of speculation, which keep the mind constantly on the stretch, and which in a moment, give or take away a fortune." Reader! remember these things when drawing up your balance sheet.

CHAPTER XII

AVARICE AS AN HEREDITARY PASSION.

A puzzle for philosophers—Illustrated cases of avarice as an hereditary passion—John Elwes—Daniel Dancer—Miss Vooght—Acquisitiveness as a family failing—Brothers Jackson, the Two Misers of Reading— Brothers Palmer, the Two Misers of Witney—Old Jardine, the Miser of Cambridge, and his two sons; a singular instance of avarice as a family vice, &c.

AVARICE AS AN HEREDITARY PASSION.

There are few subjects upon which it is so difficult to form an opinion as that of the hereditary nature of the human passions. There are few subjects that have so puzzled philosophers, and few that have so effectually baffled the sagacity of science. There is one point which has been satisfactorily proved, viz. that if the qualities of the human mind are hereditary, they are not always derived from the father. But this fact adds to the perplexity of the question, inasmuch as it becomes necessary, before we advance facts against the doctrine of the hereditary nature of the human feelings, to ascertain as to the peculiar disposition and temperament of both parents. Thus, the fact of a miser begetting a generous and noble-hearted son, is no proof that he might not have derived these good qualities as an hereditary birthright from the mother. Corroborative illustrations therefore, are of more weight, since we have less difficulty in applying them, and tracing the analogy between the disposition of the parent, and the disposition of the child. The force of example, it may be said, may have much to do with quickening this passion into life; but an example not the most prepossessing, could never be so warmly embraced had not the natural inclinations a tendency to hoard, and to coincide with the habits of the miser.

The reader will perhaps remember among our examples the

case of John Overs, whose daughter was so unlike the father; or that of John Mounsey, whose son manifested so generous a disposition: but it must be remembered, that in neither case have we any information relative to the disposition of the mother. Our facts which bear on the other side of the question are somewhat stronger. That of Daniel Dancer, and his sister; of the three Misses Vooght, and of the Elwes', are singular instances of acquisitiveness as a family failing. The family of the Dancers were notoriously parsimonious, and were all eager and covetous after gold. Miss Dancer equalled her brother in the art of saving; and another brother who survived this miserly pair for many years, is said, if such a thing could be possible, to have been eyen more penurious than Daniel Dancer himself.[1]

The case of John Elwes is one deserving of some attention; for when we learn that the mother of Elwes was an example of penury almost unequalled by her son; that with one hundred thousand pounds which she possessed from her husband, she literally starved herself to death; and when moreover we learn that Sir Harvey Elwes her brother, was one of the most extraordinary misers on record, who, to amass wealth spent sixty years of his life in a state of seclusion which an ancient Coenobite might have envied: we cannot but regard the life of John Elwes as a singular and memorable fact, to substantiate the doctrine of the innateness and hereditary nature of the human passions. In the lives of some misers, we have seen this propensity to acquire engrossing all other feelings, captivating, as it were the very soul; but in Elwes we observe some good qualities; signs of generosity, and a proneness to forgive injuries at which other men would have been unmerciful. His life in fact, is a record of constant strugglings and wrestlings between passions, which at first sight appear inconsistent, as the promptings of one mind, and which we should scarcely believe

1. Annual Register, Vol. XXXVI., for the year 1794

could exist in the same man, did not science and experience teach us how incongruous are the propensities of the human mind.

The indication of avarice sometimes observed in infancy and youth would lead us to believe in the innateness of the human propensities. All who have been in the habit of observing the gradual opening of youthful minds—all who have devoted their energies to the education of the rising generation, must have observed how powerfully will the spirit of covetousness sometimes sway the actions of youth, long before the vices or the cunning of the world could have excited such feelings; and will, on reading the following lines of Crabbe, call to mind the remembrance of many with whom they have come in contact:

Lo! one who walks apart although so young
He lays restraint upon his eyes and tongue;
Nor will he into scrape or dangers get,
And half the school are in the stripling's debt;
Suspicious, timid, he is much afraid
Of trick or plot,—he dreads to be betrayed;
He shuns all friendship, for he finds they lend,
When lads begin to call each other friend.

Crabbe's Borough.

Of acquisitiveness as a family failing, the case of John and James Jackson is a curious illustration. These two misers lived during the middle of the last century at a village in the vicinity of Reading. At the age of twenty they each became possessed of riches. Their passion to acquire was too strong to allow them to enjoy these acquisitions, and their only pleasure was in hoarding up, and scraping to add to their abundant store. Riches, instead of a blessing, became in their hands a curse. From principles of economy, and from congeniality of disposition, they both lived together. They hired one miserable dirty room, into which for fifty years no human being except themselves was allowed to enter: they lived so penuriously that they denied themselves the necessaries of life; and their appearance was so squalid, that passengers in the streets bestowed their charity upon them, which these unworthy wretches were never known to refuse. Nothing could have been more sordid, and nothing more miserable, than such a life: yet perhaps by thus feeding their ruling passion, they derived some enjoyment from their existence. When at the respective ages of ninety-three and eighty-seven the two brothers were taken ill, and languishing for a week, they both died on the same day, leaving behind them an accumulation of one hundred and fifty thousand pounds.

A similar instance of fraternal misery is recorded in the Cambridge Chronicle of December 26, 1767. Two brothers named John and Joseph Palmer lived together in a most parsimonious manner at Witney, in Oxfordshire. Although possessing considerable wealth, they indulged themselves in no comforts—inhabited a wretched attic—kept no servant—wore rags instead of clothes, and in their domestic arrangements were prodigies of filth and penury. They were both bachelors, and detested even the very sight of women; they would never permit one to clean out their chamber; and as they never took the trouble to fulfil that duty themselves, their apartment was a harbour for vermin, and a receptacle for dust and rubbish. In April 1767 they were both taken ill; and as in the case just quoted above, both died on the same day within a few minutes of each other. Having dwelled together in life, they were not separated in death.

Many years ago, there lived, at Cambridge, a miserly old couple of the name of Jardine: they had two sons, the father was a perfect miser, and at his death one thousand guineas were discovered secreted in his bed. The two sons grew up as parsimonious as their sire. When about twenty years of age, they commenced business at Cambridge as drapers; and they continued there until their death. During forty years, they never had their house cleaned but once, and that was on the occasion of their mother's death. They were strangers to filial love, and the loss of a parent produced no sorrow. They begrudged the last tribute of affection; and, to save a trifling fee, they laid out the corpse themselves, and bargained for her interment on the lowest scale. The establishment of the Messrs. Jardine was the most dirty of all the shops in Cambridge. Customers seldom went in to purchase, except perhaps out of curiosity. The brothers were most disreputable looking beings; for although surrounded with gay apparel, as their staple in trade, they wore the most filthy rags themselves. It is said that they had no bed, and, to save the expence of one, always slept on a bundle of packing cloths under the counter. In their housekeeping they were penurious in the extreme. A joint of meat did not grace their board for twenty years. They always had an eye to business; and if a shopkeeper or a farmer happened to purchase of them, they would enquire their address, and go a mile or two to purchase of them in return a few eggs or half a pint of beer; yet they always observed the utmost caution, lest, as they used to observe, any of their other customers should be offended. When the first of the brothers died, the other, much to his surprise, found large sums of money which had been secreted even from him. They both died suddenly and within a few months of each other. They left about eight thousand pounds, the whole of which, with the exception of a twenty pound legacy, was left to a neighbour, who, on one or two occasions had shown them some little kindness, and sent them now and then a dinner.

We do not pretend, from these facts, to build a theory or to maintain a new doctrine: we offer them simply as facts and illustrations, which may be useful in forming an opinion. We do not pretend to think them sufficient to prove the passion of avarice hereditary, but we regard them as examples of some weight in favour of that opinion. We would, in short, rather that our readers judged for themselves, than that we should point out the way that we would have them judge. The subject is a difficult one, and we think it rash and somewhat unseemly to decide prematurely upon that, which so many great men have been unable to decide, and so many philosophers have been unable to prove.

CHAPTER XIII

MAMMON WORSHIP; ITS SACRIFICES AND REWARDS.

Love of Speculating—The Tulip Mania in Holland—The South Sea Stock bubble; its origin, &c.—Its demoralizing influence—The Railway Mania—Illustrations of avarice—Anecdote from Madame de Genlis of a miser and a Surgeon—Sacrifices of the parsimonious—The rewards of Mammon, &c.

MAMMON WORSHIP; ITS SACRIFICES AND REWARDS.

With the advancement of science and the progress of civilization, the general tone of society has not proportionately improved. The age abounds with many illustrations of progress, of vast enterprize—of genius and of talent. But the mainspring of all this activity—of all these gigantic schemes, admirable inventions, and discoveries, is evidently the love of gain. Napoleon designated us a nation of shopkeepers; could he now describe us, he would designate us a nation of speculators; competition has rendered the usual course of trade inadequate to satisfy ambition, and men look eagerly for some speculation by which their riches may be augmented with greater speed, they enter into any scheme however wild, and into any project however improbable; some few grow rich on the ruin of the many, and votaries of Mammon become more numerous. If we call to mind the bubbles which at various times have excited the cupidity of avarice, we shall be surprised that men have not learnt in their failure a little wisdom to protect them against such fascinations for the future. The tulip mania, which raged among the Dutch in the year 1634, will show how the reason will become dazzled with the hope of gain. We regard now, that singular infatuation as a species of madness; and we can scarcely credit, although the fact is well authenticated, that men could have been so absurd as to invest four thousand florins in the purchase of a single bulb. A tulip, called the Admiral Liefken was worth, at the market value, four thousand four hundred florins; and the Semper Augustus produced five thousand five hundred florins in cash. Holland was the El Dorado of enthusiasts. In 1636 the tulip mania was at its height: regular offices were established in the cities of Holland. Stock jobbers were seized with the prevailing epidemic, dealt largely in tulips, and they became a favorite species of stock, and every one was eager to invest their fortunes in Dutch bulbs; men threw up their trade, and rushed to the tulip marts with their capital. The wealthy parted with houses and broad lands for a few bulbs. Legitimate trade was neglected, and the public mind was in a continual ferment; every day reports reached the ears of anxious tradesmen and poor artisans of some ease of sudden fortune, of some needy man made rich by the lucky speculation of a day. Laws were drawn up with legislative gravity for the due regulation of tulip dealers, and tulip buyers; and every one seemed to be convinced that the golden trade in tulips would last for ever. By and bye when they had their tulips instead of lands and tenements; instead of cash in the funds, or capital in trade, some few found a time to think—thought soon restored the reason, and cooled the brain; and those who were wise enough to think, made speedy sales. There were more tulips, but fewer buyers—the bubble burst—a panic spread, and thousands mourned over ruin and desolation—over cheerless homes, and beggared prospects—the once ample fortune of many an opulent merchant—of many a thriving trader, and comfortable artisan, was now contained in a few bulbs, which no one cared to buy. The South Sea bubble is another lamentable instance of the spirit of avarice as displayed in speculation. This company, as our readers are doubtless aware, was first proposed in the year 1711, and was founded upon the supposition, that the English would be allowed to trade to the coast of Peru. In the year 1720, the scheme was brought before the public. Sir John Blunt drew up the plans, and submitted them to the Chancellor of the Exchequer, A company was formed, and a bill brought before parliament. By circulating favourable reports, the project soon excited the attention of the public. For five days the books of the company were opened for a subscription of one million, at the rate of three hundred pounds for every hundred pound of capital. Eager crowds came to invest their money; in a few days the stock was worth three hundred and fifty per cent, and it ultimately rose to one thousand pounds. The rage for speculation now commenced; new companies started up every day, with schemes as chimerical as the South Sea delusion. Some, in fact had no scheme at all; and actually issued prospectuses, and solicited subscriptions for a stock, the intention and purpose of which they did not condescend to explain; one cunning rogue pretended that he had discovered a plan, by which fortune would be certain to follow; he promised to publish the particulars in a month; in the meantime, two guineas were to be paid to entitle the person to a subscription of one hundred pounds. The project, wild as it was, was not too wild for the age; one thou- sand dupes paid in one day their first instalment, and the next day the swindler had decamped. This spirit of speculation was soon to be at an end. The noble and the wealthy, royalty and the poor, bishops, clergymen, doctors, authors, merchants, and artisans, all dabbled in the South Sea Stock, during the memorable year 1720. But one day in September the stock suddenly fell; fear filled every heart, and every one rushed into the mart with their stock; on the 29th, it went down from one thousand per cent to one hundred and fifty. Merchants closed their warehouses, and bankers in disguise sought refuge in other kingdoms. Numbers were ruined passed all redemption; despair, insanity, or suicide, was the fate of thousands; and the public morals, and the course of commerce and industry, received a check which it took years to overcome.

Such are the delusions which the avarice of a people will sometimes lead them into. We might easily produce other examples; we might point to the era of lotteries, and show their demoralizing influence on society. In recent times—in the spurious companies of the year 1826, and in the railway mania of the last few years, we might also point to striking illustrations of this Mammon worship, and of the wild enthusiasm of Mammon's votaries.

But this eager pursuit of wealth too often entails misery and retribution. It is a significant fact, that in times of such adventure and speculation cases of insanity are very numerous, and the bills of mortality exhibit a fearful increase. The alternate hopes of a golden future, and the fear of beggary and ruin, haunt the fevered mind both day and night; and when disappointment comes, as it too often does, with loss of fortune and loss of peace, the infatuated worshipper of Mammon sinks into a premature grave, or broods over his loss with a mind in which the light of reason is no more.

Such are the effects of avarice as exemplified in the spirit of gambling and speculation; and we have seen, in our previous chapters, the effects of avarice as exemplified in the spirit of parsimony. The one will sacrifice to Mammon, wealth, in the hopes of future golden blessings; the latter will sacrifice health, comfort, and the soul, to retain that which he has already received. Rather than part with his gold, we have seen the miser die of actual starvation; and in the cases of Sir William Smyth and Vandille it has been shown how insignificant is pain or the fear of danger to the miser, when compared with the torture which he feels at parting with his hoards.

Madame de Genlis relates a curious anecdote in her "Souvenirs de Felicie L***," of a rich miser, curiously illustrating the sacrifices which avarice will make to Mammon. M. de C*** was very rich, but had become blind by a cataract which had formed on both his eyes; he dwelled in the remotest part of Languedoc, and he went to Paris to consult a surgeon, who told him that he must be couched, for the success of which he would be answerable. M. de C*** enquired what would be the expense of the Operation. "Fifty livres," replied Graujean. M. de C*** loudly remonstrated against the charge, which he protested was enormous, and offered to make a bargain to lower the price; the surgeon was inflexible, and with an ill grace M. de C*** was compelled to submit. Some days afterwards the surgeon completed the operation on one eye, when having removed the bandages, M. de C*** exclaimed with transport that his sight was perfectly restored. "Come then," said the oculist, "let us proceed to the other eye." "Stay," replied the miser, "you ask fifty guineas for the whole operation, that is five-and-twenty for each eye; now as I see quite as well as is necessary, I shall content myself with one eye; to pay so much for the other would be extravagance, seeing that it would be a luxury only: there are your five-and-twenty guineas!"

For these sacrifices, what are the rewards of Mammon worship? We refer to the lives of those miserable objects of self-inflicted penury, which we have related in our former chapters, as a fit answer to such a question. Youth without the joys of youth, manhood without the purposes and duties of life, old age without one ray of solace or consolation, and death on a squalid bed of misery, unattended and unbedewed with the tear of affection, are the rewards which Mammon vouchsafes to his anxious followers.

CHAPTER XIV

CONCLUSION.

The Lives of Misers teach us that no propensity can be abused without entailing its own punishment—The Effects of Avarice—Its appearance in Youth—Manhood—and Old Age—Concluding Remarks, &c.

CONCLUSION.

We imagine that the most inquisitive will not be dissatisfied at the scantiness of our facts. We have given more perhaps, than some will care to read, but we have not given them without feeling assured that they will be found useful to others than those, who merely seek amusement from their perusal. We flatter ourselves that as delineations of the human mind, as manifestations of the abuse of one of the propensities of our nature, they may prove instructive to the philosopher. The phrenologist will find among our anecdotes many illustrations, and perhaps many corroborations of his science. It was the doctrine of Gall and Spurzheim that no mental power could be abused or rendered over excited by immoderate gratification, without entailing its own punishment as a necessary consequence; and certainly in the wretched lives, in the pining, anxious, endless cares; in the remarkable deaths of the votaries of avarice whose lives and vices we have endeavoured to display, we observe, an awful retribution follow their sins against nature's laws.

Some of our examples would seem to favour this doctrine of the innateness of the human passions; for the passion of avarice is found peeping forth in infancy, triumphant in manhood, all-absorbing in old age, and sometimes strong in death. It is observed to be the most powerful when least prompted by necessity, or by the fear of future want. Abuse seems to grow with abuse—activity becomes more active when encouraged by gratification: the passion of avarice expands as it is fed. The miser with a moderate store of wealth, may feel that to double his riches, would be to satisfy his cravings; but he deludes himself: they are doubled, and with the augmentation of riches, he discovers an augmentation of desire. His first ardent wish now appears insignificant, and he feels more ambitious, more restless, and more greedy for acquisitions than ever. Gratification has fed and stimulated his avarice, and increased his ideas of wealth: he thinks himself poor, although he has doubled his fortune.

We have seen, by many deplorable examples, how the gratification of this propensity absorbs all other feelings—how the very soul, and the purposes, and duties of life are sacrificed to subdue the insatiable thirst of this inordinate passion. We have seen how the slave of avarice becomes the most despicable—the most grovelling, and the most worthless of human kind. We have seen how, when blinded by this lust for gold, affection has been extinguished; honor and rectitude have been undermined; social duties have been neglected; and domestic ties have been disregarded. We have seen how, even on the bed of death, the miser has been still greedy to acquire; how, whilst on the very threshold of that grave, which would soon render back his body to its parent earth; he has been painfully anxious to increase the heap of dross, which his avarice had already accumulated; how all thought of the endless future, all thought of the vast eternity into which he was about to enter was discarded, in gratifying in his last dying moments this ruling passion of his soul. We have seen the miser, whilst neglecting his own physical preservation, and refusing medical aid that he might save a paltry fee, hurried into eternity; and we have read that some have died, repining amidst the agonies of death, that they could not live longer to acquire more! We have in fact, seen how the miser to gratify his senseless craving for gold,

> "Throws up his interest in both worlds—
> First starved in this, then damned in that to come."

Yet, like other powers and propensities of the human mind, the propensity to acquire has its legitimate sphere of usefulness, capable of adding to the blessings and the purposes of life. To its healthy exercise we are indebted for many of those perilous enterprises which have resulted in the discovery of unknown regions, to those vast schemes of art, which have enabled us to span the world with iron roads, and to plough the deep with untiring swiftness. The love of worldly gain, honorably and nobly made manifest, will act sometimes as a lever to lift the soul to gigantic efforts, and to stimulate the sleeping brain to effusions of immortal worth. God gives us the elements of mental action, but has left it to ourselves to train by education, these elements into a virtuous and honorable course. If we totally neglect the propensity, to acquire, we become the spendthrift; if we exert it into undue activity we become the miser. Observation and science would lead us to imagine that some are born with a preponderance of this propensity; whilst others are only endowed with a moderate share. If such observations are correct—if the deductions drawn from these facts are true, the responsibilities of education are doubled. It becomes the solemn duty of the monitor of youth to discourage that propensity in the one, by displaying the sinfulness of avarice and to encourage prudence in the other, by teaching how necessary is economy in the affairs of life.

And now, in parting, we cannot but express a hope that we have done something more than amuse the curious reader. We shall feel well repaid if we have done this; for we look upon it as a pleasant thing to make ourselves pleasant unto others; but we hope that whilst exciting a smile on the countenance, we may also have aroused a better feeling in the heart, have made our readers less prone to regard so tenaciously their hoards, and to have sown a disposition within them to bestow in charity a part of that of which they may have an abundance. We should, indeed, be amply repaid if our little book should be the means of converting one soul from the idolatry of Mammon to the faith of brotherly love, if it should be instrumental in softening one heart, which had become hardened by avarice; or if it should be the cause of inspiring one poor but improvident man with the wish to save, or one rich, but avaricious man, with the desire to give. It is indeed, a great thing in the eyes of the world to be a man of wealth; but it is a still greater thing in the sight of heaven, to be a man of charity.

FINIS.

Printed in Great Britain
by Amazon

15454622R00105